Bill:
Thanks very much
for buying Rally!
I really hope
you enjoy it.

Yours in Notre Dame,

Jeff Jeffanu

RALLYE

RALLY!

The 12 Greatest
Notre Dame
Football Comebacks

Jeff Jeffers

ICARUS PRESS
South Bend, Indiana
1981

Rally!
The 12 Greatest Notre Dame Football Comebacks
© 1981 Jeff Jeffers

Icarus Press, Inc.
Post Office Box 1225
South Bend, Indiana 46624

1   2   3   4   5   6   7   8   9   10   84   83   82   81

Library of Congress Cataloging in Publication Data

Jeffers, Jeff, 1953-
    Rally! : the 12 greatest Notre Dame football
comebacks.

    Includes index.
    1. University of Notre Dame—Football—History.
I. Title.
GV958.U54J43   796.332'63'0977289   81-7195
ISBN 0-89651-651-2   AACR2

To my parents: My father, who taught me about the game of football and of life, and my mother, who taught me to read and write proper things in a proper manner.

To J. G. Ruyle: A great example of not quitting even when your entire adult life has been a comeback against staggering odds.

And to the men and women who have been, who are and who will be the University of Notre Dame.

CONTENTS

ACKNOWLEDGEMENTS

The effort to write a book as this is not accomplished without a great deal of support from very special and kind people.

The management and staff of the WNDU Stations have been family to me for the past six years. Our tears, joys, victories and defeats have been a shared experience.

It is not easy to adequately express my thanks to those people at Notre Dame who assisted me during the preparation of the manuscript. Roger Valdiserri, John Heisler and Karen Croake run one of the best sports information offices in the country. Their friendship was as needed as were certain pictures and data.

There are many who, when they learned of *Rally!*, were more than enthusiastic and supportive. Mike Collins, Jeff and Cathy Ray, Jim Corgel, John Sparks, Jim Bognar, Tom Dennin, Tim McDevitt, Armando Femia, Fr. Jim Riehle, John Pastor, George and Gloria Kelly, Greg and Bern Blache, Pauline and Myron Busby, and Brian and Micki Boulac were extremely gracious with their time and patience. Even the legendary John Gaski had a few good things to say.

Bruce Fingerhut and Jeanne Krier of Icarus Press and Notre Dame Press respectively put a great deal of time and labor into *Rally!* It is both personally and professionally enjoyable to work with them.

I would be remiss if I did not mention some of the people in the athletic department at Notre Dame who were more than gracious with their time and interest. The athletic directors, Moose Krause and Gene Corrigan, along with associate director Col. Jack Stephens have always been more than cooperative. Former head coaches Ara Parseghian and Dan Devine along with members of their staffs were invaluable in the recollection of events and details.

The limitations of space excludes some people who were instrumental in this book. But it is hoped that whatever degree of enjoyment they gain from *Rally!* will be taken as a token of my sincere thanks.

FOREWORD

We were standing on the carpet just behind the end zone in the Cotton Bowl. It was a most unusual place for sports writers to be in the closing minutes of a thrilling football game, but this was a most unusual afternoon. We were on the carpet because there was less likelihood of being afflicted by frost-bitten toes than if we waited on ice-glazed concrete.

Joe Mooshil, midwest sports editor for Associated Press and a man whose sulphurous language sometimes melts icicles, turned to me and said, "Well, you redheaded (censored), it looks like you're going to be (censored) right again."

"Not yet," I shouted into the norther that was whipping through the stadium. "Don't say that yet. The way this insane game is going I have a hunch you're going to be right."

Eight days earlier Mooshil and I had been warm, comfortable and dry as we lounged in luxurious Studio A at WGN radio in Chicago. That afternoon we had made predictions of the outcome of the incredible event unfolding before our ice-crusted eyelids.

We agreed on one point. Notre Dame vs. Houston in the 1979 Cotton Bowl game would be a wild, high-scoring game. I picked Houston "something like 33–31." Mooshil, a very precise and positive Assyrian, said, "Notre Dame, 35–34."

1

We were in the end zone, en route to what we hoped would be warm dressing rooms, because nobody cared about us being within the field of play. Almost nobody was there to care. The two football squads probably outnumbered the thoroughly frozen nuts still in the stands. It was like watching a game between neighborhood teams in the glorious era of "prairie football" in Chicago.

I was reminded of Babe Ruth's classic putdown of football players. "Baseball players have sense enough to come in out of the rain," the Bambino had said. The Babe would not have believed this football game. Nobody south of the Arctic Circle ever had played football in such deplorable weather.

Mooshil was covering his first Cotton Bowl game, but he had known in advance that Dallas was no winter resort. What nobody except God and Knute Rockne could have known was that Dallas would be paralyzed by a rare ice storm that turned the weird ramps at the Dallas-Fort Worth airport into bobsled runs. And turned the Cotton Bowl carpet into a skating rink.

"These guys must have (censored) Eskimo blood in their veins," Mooshil speculated as he peered at 22 players skidding and sliding under a vaporous cloud created by their frozen exhalations.

Notre Dame, trailing 34–12 with less than eight minutes to play, had stormed (and I use the word advisedly) back to 34–28 at 4:22. They had been brought back by flu-shaking quarterback Joe Montana, who at halftime had done his male impersonation of Garbo playing the death scene in "Camille."

With 35 seconds left, Mooshil conceded to me. "You called this one," he hollered through the gale after Houston got the "final" break of the game, an Irish offsides that cancelled an 11–yard punt by Houston and restored the ball to the Cougars. With inches to go at Houston's 49, its coach, Bill Yeoman, wisely decided to go for it on fourth down rather than risk a center snap to his punter being intercepted by an Irish figure skater.

"They're not going to make it," I bellowed back. And they didn't. There is no need for me to supply the rest of it. Jeff

Jeffers handles that nicely in this memorable book of memorable comebacks.

I especially thank Jeff for having the good taste to include some of those games in which the valiant Irish shook down the thunder but didn't quite win over all. Jeff makes us understand that losing gallantly can be beautiful, too. This is a book to warm us all during cold nights in South Bend, Chicago and . . . Dallas.

—BILL GLEASON
Chicago Sun-Times

INTRODUCTION

After one stirring Notre Dame comeback a football fan, with no particular interest in the Irish or any other college team, asked me why Notre Dame always seems to rally and win when all is apparently lost.

That question set the works in motion for this book. The question, like most inquiries about Irish football, is both simple and complex. The following words and pictures will hopefully answer the question by citing examples of the phenomenon known as "The Notre Dame Comeback."

There is not a college in the country that has not staged a rally that produced a win in the face of long odds. Why then do Irish comebacks merit special attention?

The credit and/or blame for this can be traced to one Knute Kenneth Rockne, N.D. '14. Rockne projected Notre Dame football to the international plateau it has occupied since his coaching days. Since the time of Rockne, everything with anything associated with Irish football has been magnified to enormous proportions. Every win is seen by some as a victory for all that is right while each defeat is a crushing, gut-wrenching debacle that must be endured for at least seven days. Each coach who has trod the sidelines at Notre Dame has had to live in the fishbowl that comes with the job. The pressure, anxiety, exhilaration and trauma take their toll.

A Notre Dame football fan sees the team as his or her own. A squad for which to live and die. There is no middle ground with Irish football. The laissez-faire attitude is quickly abandoned when Notre Dame is mentioned.

There will be some who vehemently disagree, but Notre Dame has attracted a special type of football player since the sport began at the Indiana school. Coaches who have recruited against the Irish are the first to admit this. The player who comes to Notre Dame is not always the best player at his position in the nation or on the field of play. There are other schools who have fielded much better teams than Notre Dame. But over the years, Notre Dame has become synonymous with character and excellence in players, coaches and teams. The leadership of the university and the athletic department must receive credit for maintaining this high level of accomplishment.

As a high school player watches a Joe Theismann or Joe Montana stage a dramatic drive in the final quarter and gain a victory, there is a great amount of projection into the role of hero. If the scenario is repeated often enough it becomes the expected, not the unique.

Do Notre Dame football players ever give up? Of course, they are not machines. A player can give the ultimate effort in a total coordination of physical and mental ability. Some coaches refer to this exertion as the "110% factor." When an entire team performs at its highest level, then anything is possible on the field. It is during this time when great efforts and great comebacks are accomplished. When every member of a team puts the effort at a particular time in a particular situation, that is when the magic occurs. The exploits of the teams, coaches and players that follow are examples of what happens when the time, situation and circumstance lend themselves to that optimum effort and result. Not all of the comebacks resulted in victory, but the effort is what exemplifies the spirit that is college football and, Notre Dame.

1

ARMY, 1913

"The Source"

Notre Dame's first nationally recognized athletic success was almost accidental. In 1913 the University of Notre Dame was perceived as an all-male, small, midwestern school that attracted impoverished, young men of diverse, ethnic backgrounds. And Notre Dame may have stayed a quaint Catholic school with a less than grandiose future if it had not met the United States Military Academy in a football game on November 1, 1913.

Football at that time was more like rugby than today's game. The eastern style of play was characterized by heavy pushing and pulling in the line while the midwestern version featured more running to the outside and less emphasis on the physical melee.

Notre Dame had successful teams even before the 1913 game with the Cadets. In 1892 and 1893 the Irish did not lose and in 1903 they shut out all opponents. By the time of the Army game in 1913, Notre Dame's all-time record was 115 wins, 31 losses and 13 ties.

The man for whom Army's home field is named began football at West Point. Cadet Dennis Michie got together with thirty of his fellow corps members in 1890 and organized a team. Michie had no idea that the football program he began would meet Notre Dame twenty-three years later and change the game forever.

The coaches in the first great game in modern college football history came from dramatically different athletic backgrounds. Jess Harper had attended the University of Chicago where he was a substitute for Walter Eckersall. Harper had previously coached at Wabash College in Crawfordsville, Indiana, before taking on the job at Notre Dame. His coaching counterpart had a long and distinguished athletic career by the time he returned to his alma mater before the 1913 football season. Lt. Charlie Daly had been one of West Point's first All-American players. After graduation in 1905, Daly served as an army officer for one year, then resigned his commission. He coached as an assistant to Percy Haughton at Harvard in 1909 and came back to the Point to teach the Army players the strategy that had made Harvard one of the top teams in the nation.

Ironically, it was a baseball game that prompted the first football game between Notre Dame and Army. Although Notre Dame had an outstanding football record, the school was better known for its baseball teams. The football squads were recognized only on a regional basis. This reflects the national mood of the day; baseball was by far the top sport while football was seen as a ruffian game played by those who could not master a bat and ball.

Jess Harper and his team of 1913 had looked for a way to improve the team's national image. He felt he had the potential for a team that could compete with the powers of the East. In January of 1913 the two schools played a baseball game and the idea was hatched to get together in the fall for football. The problem that stood in the way of the match was the small Indiana school's precarious financial situation.

Teams that played West Point had to provide their own transportation to and from the game. Harper was not sure that the football budget could handle a trip to New York and back, so he told the Notre Dame student manager to cable the Army manager to find out about how much of the gate would be guaranteed the Irish. The Cadet manager said $600; Harper knew the return trip would cost much more but decided to take the chance. Each team member had to travel light and some stayed home. It was a motley crew that ventured to West Point in the fall of 1913.

Two of the Irish players had their lives changed forever on that first day of November in 1913. Knute Rockne was an immigrant from Norway who had heard about Notre Dame while working to aid his family in Chicago. A burning desire to better himself and escape the lower working class led him to South Bend. Rockne came to Notre Dame for one reason: to get an education, and anything that stood in the way of school would be dismissed without a second thought.

But Notre Dame in 1910 had developed a Spartan aura among the students, and he who did not at least attempt to make the football team soon found himself out of the mainstream of university life. Rockne was twenty-five years old when he entered college and his maturity and athletic ability did not go unnoticed by the football coach, Shorty Longman. He had been a good track man in high school but had not played organized football. Longman gave Rockne the chance to play but the former Michigan player did not stay long at Notre Dame. The next coach was Jack Marks who groomed the young, green squad into a pretty good team. Rockne progressed as a player and found himself mentioned as a possible honors candidate for the 1913 season. Rockne faced a big decision before the 1913 school year. His father died, and he was torn between returning to school and staying at home to help support his family. After much soul searching, he decided to return to Notre Dame. He also decided to play football for the new coach, Jess Harper.

The player who had the biggest effect on Knute Rockne was a superb baseball pitcher named Charles E. "Gus" Dorais. Dorais' pitching style lent itself well to throwing the football. Coach Longman was never convinced that Dorais could make the forward pass an integral part of the Irish attack. But with Rockne catching most of his tosses, Dorais perfected the quick, accurate pass. Notre Dame used the pass for three years but still emphasized the rush. The forward pass was a novelty, a gadget to be used when all else failed. A "real football team" preferred to grind out the yardage than to utilize such a tactic.

Rockne and Dorais developed a particular type of pass that nearly always worked. During one practice session, Rockne fell as he tried to catch a Dorais toss. The duo then made the "buttonhook" a patterned play, with Rockne sliding past the defender and facing the line of scrimmage while meeting the ball in midair.

It is a widespread misconception that Notre Dame introduced the forward pass in the 1913 Army game. As noted previously, the pass had been around for a long time. What did make the game memorable was that a favored team (Army), that was covered extensively in the press, lost to a squad (Notre Dame) that was almost completely unknown in the eastern United States.

The way the game began, Notre Dame should have foregone its "noble venture" and stayed home. The men from South Bend were plainly in awe of the Army team. The "H" backfield of Hodgson, Hodges and Hobbs was one of the best in the nation. Vernon Prichard was supposedly a much more refined quarterback than Dorais, and Daly was a coach without equal among Eastern teams.

Army picks up the first break of the game when Dorais fumbles deep in Notre Dame territory and the Cadets recover. Yet Army mistakes force a punt and Dorais redeems himself with a thirty-yard runback from his own five. Dorais decides to pass. He has decent field position and knows Army would not expect it. Rockne is wide open, but the pass is overthrown. The Irish punt but Dorais shanks his kick, and Army takes possession at midfield.

Daly's team makes no yardage and Hodgson punts back to Notre Dame. Once again the more powerful and physical Cadet team dominates, and Notre Dame fumbles. Still the defense holds, and Army must punt again. This style of play

Notre Dame team, 1913. Captain Knute Rockne holds ball with quarterback Gus Dorais at his left. Coach Jess Harper is at upper right, top row.

sounds boring, but the game of ebb-and-flow football was the rule in 1913.

Notre Dame seems to be playing its best football in a long

time. The turnovers have cost the Irish dearly, and the crowd senses that the superior Army team would soon control the game. Notre Dame, already much thinner than the Cadets in players, is taking a beating. Rockne has hurt his leg and is limping around the field. Notre Dame is hanging tough, but that's about it.

Dorais calls for a long pass pattern on the next Notre Dame possession. Rockne suddenly finds a cure for his ailing limb and gets behind the Army defenders, and the Irish draw first blood. The all-around-athlete Dorais kicks the extra point, and it's 7–0.

The visitors' touchdown seems to infuriate Army. Hodges and Hobbs plunge through the line for big gains and Prichard hits Jack Jouett with a pass as Army moves the ball at will against a weary Notre Dame team. Hodgson tallies the first Cadet score but a missed placement makes it 7–6.

Notre Dame receives the kickoff and fumbles. Army recovers and quickly moves in for another touchdown. Prichard's passes advance the ball closer to the goal. Notre Dame makes a valiant stand against the onslaught of the Army backs but finally gives way as Johnny McEwan charges into the line and Prichard follows him into the end zone. Hoge kicks it true, and Army goes ahead, 13–7.

There is little time left in the first half and most observers think Notre Dame will run out the clock, try to heal during the intermission and keep it close in the second half. But this November afternoon is not ordinary and conventional strategy is thrown to the wind.

A not-too-sly sneak by Dorais lends credence to the belief that Notre Dame is content to trail by six after two quarters. Then Dorais fades to pass, Rockne is covered, but Joe Pliska slips open and takes the toss. What is known today as a "safety valve" pass becomes a thirty-yard gain as Pliska twists his way into Army territory. In one of the first two-minute offensive drills in football history, Dorais moves his team closer. He hits Rockne on two lofty throws and connects with Pliska on quick, hard bullets that are caught just beyond the line of

scrimmage. Army tries to adjust. Their defense is stretched
nearly the entire width of the field. This leaves them lighter in
the line, and Notre Dame takes advantage of that.

Pliska runs at the weaker defense and goes over for a score.
Dorais drops one through the uprights, and the visitors
surprisingly lead by one at half.

Both teams used the forward pass in the first and second
periods. In Army's patterns the receiver catches the ball while
standing still, then he runs. But Notre Dame's receivers, in the
midwestern styles, are running in full stride when they meet
the ball. The round shape of the ball does not encourage the
passing attack. This makes Dorais' accomplishments even
more amazing. His command of the game, in running, passing
and play calling, is rarely seen in a single player in 1913.

Notre Dame receives the second-half kickoff but can't
score. Army plays what is an ancestor of the 5–2 defense
used in the 1970s to stop the triple option. The ends play
wider, there is more room in the middle of the field, and the
secondary must honor the pass as well as the run. The Cadets
hold and get the ball back on their own twenty.

An overlooked aspect of the game is the way the Indiana
team plays on defense. Players go both ways (offense and
defense) and the extra running on the pass plays does not
seem to tax either Rockne or the other receivers when they
face the Army attack. But size and experience begin to take
effect. West Point moves the ball deeper into Irish territory, and the fans at Cullum Hall Field know it is but a
matter of seconds before Army will score. A penalty against
Notre Dame moves the ball to the Irish two where it is first
and goal.

At this point an inner force that will come back to Irish
teams time and time again comes to the fore. An Army touchdown at this point in the game would not be disastrous for
the visitors. The contest would still be close and anything
other than a rout could be seen as a "moral victory" for
Harper's team. But a tough, gut-checking defense denies
Army the score. Dorais again makes the big play as he intercepts a pass in the end zone for a touchback.

After the Dorais interception the game's momentum shifts. The Irish now set out to make a respectable showing into a historical event.

A ball control offense seems to be in order. Leading 14–13, the offense may try to consume time on the clock and keep the ball away from the Cadet offense which has consistently moved against Notre Dame. But Gus Dorais has other ideas.

He turns on his aerial radar and begins an all-out blitz of the stunned Army defense. The drive that ended with the end-zone interception took a lot out of the Cadets and running to keep up with Rockne, "Gus" Gushurst and Pliska leaves Army confused, confounded and a team on the run.

When the defense adjusts, Dorais hands off to Ray Eichenlaub who scores the final two Notre Dame touchdowns on short runs. Army stays in the game by moving the ball every chance it has, but the twenty-one points in the final quarter make any possibility of a Cadet rally only a dream of the Army officers in the crowd.

The final score was 35–13. Surprisingly the game was not then considered a turning point in the history of football. Army fans saw the upset as a bad day for their team that could be avenged at any time if the two met again. Notre Dame players were justifiably elated, but a degree of incredulity had to be present in their minds. They had just whipped one of the top college teams of the day. On the road. Away from South Bend.

Newspapers from New York, Washington, Boston and Buffalo saw the game as a lead for the Sunday morning editions. The mighty Army team had fallen to a bunch of nobodies from the hinterland. A diehard football fan knew better, but as has been noted, the game of college football was not that well known. What was known was that the U.S. Military Academy rarely lost. Victory was taught to be a way of life at West Point.

A city such as New York in 1913 teemed with immigrants who hungered for a piece of the American pie. The Irish, Italian, Polish and German communities, still dominated by the parish, suddenly had an identification outlet. Rockne came from Norway. Fitzgerald, Feeney, Keefe and Finegan had all started for this strange school that no one had heard about until the 35–13 victory.

The 1913 Notre Dame team finished the season unbeaten. But the final three wins did not have nearly as much effect as did the drubbing of Army. Students cheered as the team got off the train in South Bend. Suddenly Notre Dame football was a new institution in American sports. The small school from Indiana that played wide-open, passing football had beaten the Army in a way that made football exciting to watch. The Notre Dame football players began to attract more national attention. Dorais and Eichenlaub were named All-American. Notre Dame could now decide where they wanted to play and who they wanted to play. Army, Nebraska, Purdue and Southern California soon appeared regularly on the Irish schedule.

Gus Dorais went on to coach at Loras (in 1914 the Iowa college was known as Dubuque) and then enlisted in the Army to serve in World War I. His war-time record was compiled in Waco, Texas, where he served as sports director. In 1919 he returned to Notre Dame and coached the Irish backfield. One of Dorais' freshman runners was a young man named George Gipp. Dorais moved on to Gonzaga University where he coached football and served as athletic director. He had earned a law degree at Notre Dame but never practiced. He later entered politics, serving on the Detroit city council.

Most members of the Army team went on to active service. The United States entered the World War in 1917, and Charlie Daly was called to active duty. But the rivalry continued and still exists today.

The other star in the game went on to a life that is granted to few. Knute Kenneth Rockne took over as head coach at Notre Dame in 1919. He remained at his alma mater teaching chemistry and helping Harper with the team. He ascended to the head coaching job and became a legend.

His success at coaching was a continuance of his outstanding play. Rockne molded, twisted, cajoled and influenced people all over the world. Always with a smile and a quick wit.

The win over Army projected Notre Dame into the spotlight of the sporting world of the Roaring Twenties. Not only was the football team never to be the same, neither was the university. Nor was the game of college football. In a larger sense the defeat of Army began a feeling, an esprit de corps on the campus, that has renewed itself in trying times at least eleven more times over the next sixty-seven years.

2

OHIO STATE, 1935

"Perhaps the Greatest"

Notre Dame football probably changed more from 1913 to 1935 than during any other period in the school's history.

One tragic moment caused the greatest change. It occurred when Knute Rockne was killed in a plane crash on March 31, 1931. A terrible twist of fate took the man who had come to symbolize Notre Dame football and put an end to new chapters in the Rockne legend.

But even in death that legend continued to cast a long shadow. Seldom was Notre Dame football mentioned or written about without a reverential reference to Rockne.

Whether this helped Irish teams of this era is debatable. The romantic images of departed heroes cannot be constantly conjured for the sake of nostalgia and have effect. Rockne only asked one team to "go out and win one for the Gipper."

After Rockne's death, University administrators seriously considered de-emphasizing football. The program had been identified almost solely with his name. It seemed inconceivable that the teams after Rockne could achieve the success of his teams.

But former Rockne players Hunk Anderson and Elmer Layden were able to maintain the excellence that had become expected of Irish teams. And while there was a slight decline in support following the disaster of 1931, the threatened de-emphasis never took place.

The lure of Notre Dame still attracted fine players and huge crowds wherever the team played. Many of those attending the games initially had been drawn to Irish football by the popular Rockne. Although he was gone, Notre Dame remained the object of their affection.

Layden had no superstar in 1935, but the team was one of the most talented ever to play at Notre Dame. Two players, Bill Shakespeare and Wayne Millner, were later accorded All-America honors. But they were never as highly regarded as Gipp or the Four Horsemen.

The 1935 team posted a so-so record. Yet it is considered one of the best teams in the school's history. The team's reputation comes mainly from one game—a game that later was judged by some as the best of college football's big games.

Notre Dame was set to play Ohio State in Columbus on November 2. Both teams were expected to be among the best in the nation and had lived up to the pre-season prognostications. The winner would have the inside track on the national championship.

Francis Schmidt coached the Buckeyes in much the same way as Woody Hayes coached his great Ohio State teams. Big, strong and fast running backs pounded away at defensive lines until resistance faded. That was the basic style of football in 1935 and although more refined, has remained Ohio State's style for more than forty years. Schmidt's team mixed their powerful running game with laterals and quick pitches to make sure their speed complemented their straight-ahead force.

Notre Dame did not have Ohio State's brute power, but relied on the guile and talent of several small, quick players. Despite their small size, Shakespeare, Andy Pilney, Wally Fromhart and Millner could play physical football with anyone on the Irish schedule—except perhaps with the Buckeyes. To have a chance in the game, Notre Dame had to utilize the speed of the Irish backs to the utmost.

Layden's team swept through their first games relying on a balance of quickness and defense that gained a lot of attention among sportswriters around the country.

The contest received much pre-game press attention because for years the teams had been trying to schedule each other but had never been able to agree on a date. To the de-

The coach of the 1935 Irish squad, Elmer Layden, a member of the Four Horsemen backfield and the MVP of the 1925 Rose Bowl game.

light of fans they finally settled their differences. The match was a natural: Two teams from the heartland of America with great traditions and a great following. Football fans from all over the country would finally see the "Scarlet Scourge" and the "Fighting Irish" meet.

Chet Grant was the backfield coach for the Irish in 1935. He currently resides in South Bend, where he has written several books and is the unofficial resident sports historian at Notre Dame. In his eighties, he is as quick and alert as he was when he played running back for Rockne in 1916 and again in 1920 and 1921.

"Both teams were superbly conditioned in all areas of the game. Ohio State was the biggest team we'd face. We knew we'd have to play our best to win," recalls Grant.

In every great football game that is ballyhooed for weeks in advance, the psychological aspect becomes as important as daily practice. Both sides look for the slightest edge to gain over their opponent before the kickoff. And Layden used a little "psych job" on running back Pilney before the Irish traveled to Columbus.

Pilney had developed a reputation as a fumbler (a notion that Grant says was somewhat deserved but a little overblown). Pilney was a tremendous talent, but was plagued by the tag, "stumbler and fumbler."

Grant had worked with Pilney on holding onto the ball. This extra coaching began to take effect in the Navy game. Pilney returned several punts that put Notre Dame in good field position for scores.

In the Rockne days there sometimes appeared a short article in the *South Bend Tribune* written by "Bearskin." The coach used the alias to bring some of his haughtier players down to earth before a particularly big contest. With help from Joe Pertritz, the team's publicity man, Layden wrote a new "Bearskin" article. This one laid into Pilney and his accumulated press clippings. The "psych" job was also used on the entire team, though not in print. Layden and the coaching staff told the squad that the powerful Buckeyes would barely be taxed in the upcoming game.

The game was covered by the greats of sports journalism. Grantland Rice, Damon Runyon, Henry McLemore, Paul Gallico and Red Barber all were in Ohio Stadium for this battle of the superteams. The demand for information on the game was so great that calls for the "inside dope" ran ten to one ahead of all other calls to radio stations during the week preceding the game.

The contest also was a super game from an economic standpoint. The Great Depression had made most forms of entertainment seem frivolous for most people, yet all 81,018 seats were sold. With the expected rush on concessions and souvenirs, the total take was projected to be above $1 million.

The visitors from South Bend win the coin flip, and that's about it for Notre Dame's first half success. The Irish try to pass, but the Bucks are there to stop nearly every attempt. The big Ohio State front wall shuts down the running game. Mike Layden, the younger brother of the Irish coach, tries a pass from the 50 yard line. But Frank Antennucci intercepts. Antennucci is surrounded by Irish offensive players set to make the tackle. However, Antennucci laterals the ball to Frank Boucher, who threads his way seventy-two yards downfield and into the end zone for the score. The play is one of coach Schmidt's favorites. He often instructs his players to run for a short distance with an interception; then pass off to a free teammate. Sometimes the offense is so concerned with making the tackle that they forget about the trailing player, who takes off with the ball at full speed after catching the lateral. This time it works perfectly and the Bucks go up 7—0 following the conversion.

Notre Dame tries again to move through the air but is thwarted. Another interception gives the ball back to Ohio State. Schmidt's team drives the ball down to the Irish three and Jumping Joe Williams goes over for the second touchdown. There is no joy on the Irish side of the field. Notre Dame is down 13—0 as the first half ends.

Tim Cohane, in his recap of the game in the *NRTA Journal* (1978), focused on the halftime conversations among the sportswriters in the press box. The main topic was the awesome talent of the Buckeyes.

"I'm glad I was here to see 'em," said Runyon. "I wouldn't have believed it otherwise."

"The Ohio State team in the first half has shown me the greatest display of football I've ever been privileged to witness," commented Grantland Rice.

Paul Gallico was even more impressed, if that's possible. "It'll take Congressional action to stop those guys," he said.

But thirteen points is next to nothing for a good football team to overcome with an entire half to play. And that is the attitude in the Irish locker room. Layden does not call upon the ghost of his former coach, nor does he rant and rave over the two interceptions that led to Buckeye scores.

In his autobiography, the Irish coach recalls his halftime meeting with the team. "I felt my team needed settling down, not pepping up. We had bad breaks in the first half and we made some mistakes. As calmly as possible, I tried to discuss what we hadn't done right and should correct in the 30 minutes we had left."

At the start of the second half, two changes are made in the Irish lineup. Frank Gaul comes in at quarterback, and Pilney begins at left halfback.

There is no scoring in the third period, but Notre Dame begins to show its stuff. Pilney makes his presence felt. He slashes and bucks his way through the Buckeye line. But both defenses are tough, and the punting game is the most dominant force in the quarter. Steve Miller gets off a fine run for the Irish into Buckeye territory, but the drive stalls. Yet in the final moments of the period the Irish make a big break.

Pilney takes an Ohio State punt at his own 40 and streaks to the Bucks 13 yard line. His fumble worries behind him, Pilney has evidently responded to the extra coaching of Grant

and the sarcastic ribbing of "Bearskin." The fourth quarter begins with Notre Dame preparing for its first tally. A line plunge gains little, and the Irish go to the air. Pilney fakes a run and then throws to Gaul, who takes it on the one. Miller then lugs it over for the score, but Fromhart misses the placement and the score is 13—6.

As happens so often in a tight game, the big play by the offense inspires the defense. The consistent Buckeye offense that had pushed Notre Dame around at will in the first half cannot muster a drive. The invisible factor of momentum begins to transfer from Ohio State to Notre Dame. The home team punts to the Irish, who begin their offense on the 40.

Notre Dame comes back up the field quickly. Pilney, Fromhart, Layden and Miller take it to the Ohio State end of the field. Pilney hits Layden with a pass over the middle that carries to the one yard line. Miller tries for his second touchdown of the day but fumbles, and the Bucks recover.

Coach Grant remembers the play that apparently sealed the disappointing fate of the Irish. "You had to come down with possession in those days. If the play were made today, Miller would have been given the score, but not then."

Jim Karcher makes the big play for the Buckeye defense. Ohio State gets their fine running back Williams into the game. Jumping Joe clicks off a twenty-four yard run that nearly breaks for the score. It proves to be the last big Scarlet offensive punch of the afternoon. The Irish defense digs in and forces the punt. Three minutes remain.

Again Pilney is the main man in the Irish drive. The pass is the big weapon in the arsenal. Pilney hits Fromhart in the flat down to the Ohio State 24. A play that is as big as any in the game is made as Pilney throws for Mike Layden. It bounces off Layden's arms and into the grasp of a Buckeye defender, but he fumbles. Larry Danbom, a little used Notre Dame sub, falls on the ball, and the Irish retain possession. Pilney hits Fromhart for ten more, and Ohio State is reeling under the air attack. All four men in the backfield can throw and catch the ball. The attack is quick, surgical and strategic.

Pilney fakes a run to his right and goes for Layden in the end zone. The brother of the Four Horseman fullback goes high for the pass and brings it down for the score. But the kick is again missed. It's 13—12 in favor of the home team. There are less than two minutes remaining in the game.

It is as if two games have been played on this November afternoon. Ohio State easily won the first and is losing the second. The tough Buckeye defense, led by All-American Gomer Jones, is futilely trying to contain the Irish receivers, who are running high percentage routes that the back designated as the passer (usually Pilney) is reading well.

Every fan in the stadium knows an onside kick is coming. The Bucks recover the squib and only have to run the ball a few times, let the clock run and they will have the victory in the bag. During the entire game the Irish defense has not been able to control the Ohio State running backs. The defense has bended but not broken. Still, at this point in the game, a little bending is all that Ohio State needs to cinch the win.

The strategy is to try an end run, which would consume as much time as any play in the Buckeye playbook. The running back hopes to stay in bounds and run as far as possible from scrimmage. Dick Beltz gets the call for Schmidt's team and takes off. The Irish defense moves with Beltz and corrals him near the sideline. The ball pops free as Beltz is hit by three men. Hank Pojman, Notre Dame's second-string center, manages to touch the ball as it goes out of bounds. According to the rules of 1935 the ball goes over to the Irish. But in today's game Ohio State would still control. In 1935 the team that last touched the ball gained possession. Today's rule stipulates that the last player controlling the ball when it exits the field of play is awarded the ball.

Coach Layden sends plays into the game with his quarterbacks, Gaul and Fromhart. Pilney sweeps around end as the Irish offense begins on its own 45; he makes his way through the Bucks defense and is in the clear on the Ohio

Andy Pilney. One of many Notre Dame heroes against Ohio State in 1935.

State side of midfield. He is overtaken by several defenders at the 19 yard line. Pilney receives a crushing tackle. He leaves the game of his life with a leg injury. Andy Pilney, the butt of his coaches' "psych job" and the main hero for the Irish in this game, is through in the game of college football. This could be a giant plus for Ohio State. In addition to being rid of their number one adversary of the day, precious time ticks away as Pilney is taken off the field. The defense gets time to regain its composure, and the Irish drive is stopped for the moment.

Layden must replace Pilney. He goes with Bill Shakespeare, the best pure passer on the team. The player who will later gain All-America honors had not been in a main role due to Pilney's hot hand. But he now gets his chance. He is not as quick as the man he replaces; the Irish faithful hope his passing expertise will complete the comeback. Andy Puplis enters the game in the backfield while starting ends Millner and Marty Peters also return.

The clock shows sixty seconds to play. The pass either will give the Irish the win or simply make the fourth quarter a valiant effort.

Fromhart balks at the idea of moving the ball to the center of the field for better position to kick a field goal. A couple of line plunges would put the ball in place for a kick of thirty yards or less. But the Notre Dame kicking game hasn't succeeded all day. Fromhart knows he is leading a hot team and disdains the short-run attack.

Shakespeare's first pass from the Ohio State 19 is nearly intercepted. The clock is stopped with forty seconds left. Coach Layden looks for a quarterback to send in another play, but all are in the game. Suddenly Chet Grant pulls fourth-stringer Jim McKenna to Layden's side. McKenna had made the trip to Columbus on his own. He had to convince the stadium guards that he was a member of the Irish team. Now he leaves the bench with the play from Layden. It is a roll-out pattern that sends end Millner into the end zone, Peters and Tony Mazziotti run short routes toward the

Bill Shakespeare who threw the winning touchdown pass against Ohio State in 1935.

right sideline. McKenna, who did not log enough time in 1935 to earn a monogram, blocks Charles Hamrick (6'1", 216 pounds). And McKenna digs in with all he has to withstand Hamrick's charge.

The line picks up the rush, Shakespeare throws for Millner, who adjusts his route and heads for the pass, which is slightly behind him. Beltz and John Bettridge try to cover Millner, but he makes the catch. The Irish have scored three touchdowns in less than 15 minutes. The game ends with Notre Dame ahead, 18—13.

Red Barber, broadcasting the game across the country, had been blocked when Millner made the catch. It wasn't until his post-game show that the legendary sportscaster discovered who made the grab for the victory.

The majority of the crowd sat stunned on the banks of the Olentangy. The Irish fans who made the trip swarmed the field, while Buckeye faithful could not believe what they had witnessed.

Second half statistics indicate the Irish strength in the final quarters. Notre Dame gained only 60 yards in the first half but finished with over 400. Ohio State gained but 38 yards in the final thirty minutes against the Irish defense.

Henry McLemore of United Press said this about the action: "The 80,000 spectators who sat in on that final mad rush will never see a more savage, yet icy-cold onslaught, than Notre Dame turned on. Attacks like that come once in a lifetime."

The pre-game predictions that the winner would assuredly win the national title did not come to pass. Notre Dame lost to Northwestern the next week, 14—7. The season ended with a 6—6 tie against Army and a 20—13 win over Southern California.

The Irish had returned to the summit of the college football world. It was only for a week, but the game proved that while the memory of Rockne was something to be treasured, those who had learned from him could carry on with the same vigor and enthusiasm that had marked his regime.

Wayne Millner who made the big catch against the Buckeyes in the 1935 game.

Notre Dame beat Ohio State, 7–2, the next year. The two squads have not met since. Ohio State's Big 10 Conference schedule limits the number of non-league games that can be set up in advance. Even if the teams had been able to get together in the following years, it would've taken a pretty spectacular effort to surpass the epic struggle of 1935.

Elmer Layden understated the obvious when asked about his team's win. "It was a fine one. Yes, a fine game."

3

IOWA, 1953

"Cloud of Controversy"

Elmer Layden coached the Irish until 1941, when he was named commissioner of pro football. The former fullback, who later was inducted into the College Football Hall of Fame, finished his career at Notre Dame with a fine record of 41—10—3. His teams never lost more than two games in any year and rose as high as fifth in the national rankings.

Speculation about the identity of the next Irish coach was rampant both on and off campus. Several Notre Dame alumni were successful college coaches. They included Buck Shaw of Santa Clara, Jim Crowley of Fordham, Charley Bachman of Michigan State and Harry Stuhldreher of Wisconsin. A few votes were voiced for one Frank Leahy.

Leahy was certainly qualified for the job. In 1940 he led Boston College to an undefeated season that was capped off with a Sugar Bowl win over Tennessee. Leahy had played for Rockne, earning monograms in 1928 and 1929, but his career was hampered by injuries. It is said that Rockne recognized the great coaching potential in the youngster from Winner, South Dakota, quite early in Leahy's career.

Leahy had what is affectionately referred to as "Dome Fever." It's a malady that strikes early in life and is characterized by the unwavering belief that the University of Notre

Dame is absolutely the greatest place in the known universe. The most evident symptoms are the reluctance to leave the security of the school or, when away, the never-ending attempt to return to the comfort and tranquility of du Lac.

As soon as Leahy learned Notre Dame was seeking a new coach, he applied. By the time he first spoke with Boston College officials about getting released from his position there, he had already accepted the Notre Dame job, being chosen over Buck Shaw.

Notre Dame fans enjoyed the fruits of Frank Leahy's labor for nine years. And the Irish probably have never been as dominant on the football field as they were when Leahy coached them.

The man known as "The Master" led the Irish to four national titles and produced four Heisman Trophy winners (Bertelli, Lujack, Hart and Lattner). Leahy teams won eighty-seven, lost eleven and tied nine. But the price of success took its toll.

The end of the Leahy era probably began in 1952. The team finished with a 7—2—1 record, but it was an exasperating year for the coach. The schedule was one of the toughest in Notre Dame's history. The Irish played six league champions and managed four upsets with a squad riddled by injuries for most of the season.

The coach nearly succumbed to the pressure that his great success had built. Against Georgia Tech at Notre Dame, Leahy collapsed at halftime. He believed he was suffering a fatal heart attack. Fr. Edmund P. Joyce, Notre Dame's executive vice president, administered the last rites of the Catholic Church in the locker room. The suspected heart attack turned out to be acute pancreatitis, a condition worsened by fatigue and stress. Clearly Frank Leahy could not coach much longer for Notre Dame . . . or anybody.

Leahy knew that the end was near for him in the professional sense. He had survived in "the fishbowl" as long as he could. He led the Irish for but one more season.

"All jobs have tensions. But coaching eats out a man's insides," Leahy observed. "At Notre Dame, the pressure is worst. Not from within the school. My bosses were always telling me not to worry if we lost some games. But Notre Dame's millions of followers expect us to win."

The 1953 season saw the end of the mirth and Irish wit that had been Leahy's trademarks. The Irish that year were among the best under Leahy or any other Notre Dame head coach. Leahy himself believed his last team was his best—better even than the national champs of 1943, 1946, 1947 and 1949. Leahy's assessment may have been affected by sentimentality, but the greatness of the '53 squad is a matter of record. Better teams may have won national championships, but for individual talent that combined and meshed in an expert manner, Leahy's last team must rank among Notre Dame's best.

The roster was dotted with outstanding players. Johnny Lattner, Neil Worden, Joe Heap and Ralph Guglielmi comprised the backfield. They were much like the Four Horsemen in terms of each player being a star in his own right. Linemen Don Penza and Frank Varrichione gained All-America status before their careers ended.

Notre Dame backfield—1952. Left to right: Johnny Lattner, Neal Worden, Joe Heap, and Ralph Guglielmi.

The Irish of 1953, most of whom had received their season-ing the year before, started the season by reeling off eight straight wins in an impressive fashion. Notre Dame was rolling along as the best football team in the nation. Leahy's swan song began without a sour note. But one agonizing afternoon marred all of that. The day saw aspersions cast on Frank Leahy's character and Notre Dame's image.

All the glory that lay before the Irish was tarnished on a day that, under normal conditions, would have been re-membered as a great display of fortitude and fine clutch football.

But it was no normal day. Notre Dame's great effort was tainted by their tactics. Some called it cheating. But that is simplistic because cheating implies an evil attempt to gain by deceit. The plays in question were used by other teams, but Notre Dame was not any other team, and the plays were not used by a team in the national limelight that went with being no. 1.

Iowa was the opponent at Notre Dame Stadium this day. The Irish were favored to notch another win, but hometown fans knew it would not be a cakewalk. Iowa hoped to end its season with an upset of the country's top team. The Hawk-eyes, coached by Forest Evashevski, were 5–3 coming into the game and had nothing to lose by playing the game to the hilt. Notre Dame faced a fired-up foe that was loose and ready to play.

Iowa traditionally has upset the Irish. In 1921 Notre Dame had a twenty-two-game win streak broken by an Iowa team in Iowa City. Again in 1939, the Irish took a six-game win streak into the contest with the Hawks. The legendary Nile Kinnick was the deciding factor as Iowa won 7–6 that year. In 1940, it happened again as Notre Dame lost 7–0. The 1951 and '52 games ended in ties.

In the parlance of sport, Leahy's squad was "ripe for the taking." They were coming off an easy twenty-point win against North Carolina and were playing before a friendly crowd.

The Irish win the toss and kickoff to take advantage of the controlling wind. The Irish stop Iowa cold and Binky Broeder punts. The kick only carries eighteen yards and Notre Dame has the ball on its own 44. The Irish move a little, but an interception by Dusty Rice gives the ball back to the Hawkeyes. The ball is on the Iowa 29 as Ed Vincent gains one, then Broeder breaks off a ten-yard gain. It's Iowa's first big chunk of rushing yardage, and they go for more. Broeder gets eleven off left tackle and seven up the middle. Rice goes for ten around right end and the Irish defense reels. Iowa moves the ball to the Notre Dame 12 where Vincent skirts left end for the score. It's an eight-play, seventy-one-yard drive. James Freeman kicks the extra point, and it's 7—0, Iowa.

Notre Dame takes the kickoff and drives it down to the Iowa 32, where they turn the ball over on downs. But the Hawkeyes can't move, and Broeder punts to Heap who gets it back to his own 22.

Guglielmi now begins to move his offense. Lattner and Heap carry the ball for good gains. The drive moves the line of scrimmage to the Iowa eight yard line, where Guglielmi passes for Penza. The captain drops the ball in the end zone. Guglielmi tries again, but the drive dies as Bill Fenton, who had played superbly against the Golden Gophers of Minnesota the week before, intercepts.

But Iowa can't do anything and a punt to Lattner begins the next Irish offensive possession. The Heisman Trophy winner for the year runs it back to the Irish 41, a return of twenty-five yards. Guglielmi hits Heap out of the backfield to the Hawkeye 37. Worden grabs another down to the 25. Guglielmi again goes for Heap who makes the catch at the fourteen, even though he nearly fumbles as he comes down with the pass. Worden gains six yards over the next two carries as time dwindles in the first half. Iowa's John Hall then sacks Guglielmi. It is at this moment that controversy enters the game.

Irish tackle Frank Varrichione is still on the turf, down

with an injury. He is assisted from the field, and the clock
is stopped. When Guglielmi was tackled, only two seconds
were showing in the first half. Now there is time for one more
play. Guglielmi hits end Dan Shannon for the score. Don
Schaefer's placement is good, and the half ends with the
game tied at seven apiece.

The controversy ensues because Varrichione is not hurt
seriously and, in fact, faked the injury. But it must be
remembered that the play to stop the clock is not illegal. It is
akin to a baseball manager stalling for time when approaching
rain can possibly wash out a game in which his team is behind.
The "feigned injury" was a part of most teams' repertoire in
1953. Players played on both offense and defense, and
occasional stoppages in the game for injury and fatigue were
expected. But they did not usually directly result in the next
play being a score, nor were they usually utilized by the
nation's number one team.

The game is one of the first college football games to be
televised to a closed-circuit crowd. A group in Chicago
watching the contest broke out in uncontrollable laughter as
Varrichione was helped off the field.

In his biography of Leahy, Wells Twombley tells a story
of a practice session the week before the Iowa game. It
seems Leahy came upon Varrichione as the tackle was
practicing his "play." As Varrichione is on the Cartier Field
turf, Leahy looks down at his actor-tackle.

"Aaah no, lad," the coach says. "Better make it total
unconsciousness."

It may or may have not happened in practice. It did
happen on November 22, 1953.

The defensive teams dominate the third period. Iowa
threatens when Rice returns a Lattner punt to the Irish 33.
Broeder hits for five to the 28, but Lou Matykiewicz's pass
intended for Rice is picked off by Heap on the ten. The
quarter ends as the Irish give up the ball on downs at the
Hawkeye 29.

The fourth quarter begins with an Iowa punt to Heap.
Notre Dame carefully works the ball upfield, where

Guglielmi hits Lattner with a quick pass out of the backfield. Broeder is there for the interception on his own 48, and Iowa begins its second scoring drive.

Broeder dives for four, Rice skirts right end for three and Broeder then drives down to the Irish 42. Matykiewicz throws to Fenton to the Notre Dame seven, but the play is called back on an offsides penalty. Broeder then rips around right end for twenty-six yards to the Irish 16.

The Hawkeyes then pound it closer to the goal and score on a halfback-thrown pass from Bob Stearnes to Frank Gilliam, who makes a falling catch for the touchdown. Freeman's conversion is true and it's 14—7, Iowa.

The Iowa drive has consumed most of the fourth quarter; 2:06 remains as the Irish get the ball back. Worden sets his team in good shape as he returns the kickoff to the Notre Dame 42. Heap throws incomplete; then hits Lattner down to the Iowa 46; 1:15 remains in the game.

Guglielmi finds Lattner, who takes it down to the Hawkeye 28. Heap grabs one, and it's on the 20 of Iowa. Guglielmi, using the remaining time well, finds Lattner again down to the nine. Thirty-two seconds show on the Notre Dame Stadium clock.

Guglielmi goes for Heap in the end zone but Vincent deflects; 0:16 shows on the clock. Guglielmi passes for Heap, but it's incomplete. Six seconds remain.

Don Penza and tackle Art Hunter are down on the field. Notre Dame takes a time-out as the ailing players leave the action. Dan Shannon replaces Penza at right end. The Irish are again given another play following an injury time-out.

Leahy has dramatically engineered the drive, and the wear of the tension-filled situation shows. He is physically and emotionally spent. There is time for one play.

Guglielmi takes the snap and fakes to his left. He turns and looks across the field toward Shannon, who has broken open. Shannon makes the catch, and the Irish are within a point. Guglielmi's move, throwing "back across the grain," has capped the drive for the score.

Earlier in his career at Notre Dame, Leahy had told his

center, after the player had botched a crucial snap on a kick, that his error would cause eternal damnation. But Don Schaefer gets a fine placement and boots the extra point through as the game ends in a tie.

There were no congratulations for the superb drive that kept an unbeaten season intact. No questions were asked about the excellent play calling in the final two minutes. The objects of the reporters' queries were Varrichione and Leahy.

It is important to note that Leahy's success bred much contempt in certain circles around the country. With all his faults and failings, Leahy was entirely devoted to two things: his players and his family.

Frank Leahy saw every game as a crusade. A crusade for his team and his way of life. To Leahy, if his teams were victorious, it was because their cause was right in the quest to win. That attitude was not openly stated, but Leahy's subtle nature (at times not so subtle) infuriated many who followed college football.

There was no remorse in the Notre Dame locker room. The tactics that had saved the game from defeat were as routine as daily practice. Varrichione, as recorded in Twombley's work, was a little put off by the barrage of questions.

"No use asking because I'm not going to talk about it. I'm not saying nothing," responded the physically imposing tackle.

Irving Vaughn of the *Chicago Tribune* asked the ultimate question of Varrichione, "Were you really hurt?"

"What do you think?" stonewalled Varrichione.

The exhausted Lattner, who cinched the Heisman with his performance, was equally diplomatic.

"Pretty smart thinking, wasn't it?"

But the criticism didn't fall on the Irish until the following week. Leahy was viciously attacked in the press and letters to the university.

The letters poured into Fr. Theodore Hesburgh's and Fr. Joyce's offices. Many asked for the team to forfeit the game. Some called for Leahy's immediate dismissal. The letters sug-

1953 Heisman Trophy winner Johnny Lattner.

gested that Notre Dame did not deserve the tie and should have given the win to Iowa as a gesture of good faith and sportsmanship.

Leahy did not go with the team to Los Angeles for the annual game with Southern California. It mattered little, since the Irish romped, 48—14. The coach was back on the sideline for his final appearance at Notre Dame Stadium. His lads whipped Southern Methodist University, 40—14. The final ledger of the last year in the reign of Leahy stood at 9–0–1.

It is typical of the Notre Dame student body that they gave Leahy a triumphant exit from the field following the demolition of the Mustangs. Most who stormed the field had no idea that it was Leahy's last game. It did not matter. He was "The Master." He was their coach. Leahy was lofted off the field and carried to the locker room as the conquering hero. It was a fact that Leahy had finished at Notre Dame, but for the moment, he was the only coach for those who had sung his praises.

It is interesting to examine Leahy's reaction to the criticism that rained down on him for his player's action during the Iowa game.

"Feigned injuries have been part of the game since Walter Camp invented the first down more than seventy years ago," he said. Leahy even quoted Rockne on the subject. " 'Be sure,' Rock used to tell us, 'that the man who fakes the injury has the most capable replacement.' "

Leahy was exactly right when he explained why the feigned injury drew so much heat. He discussed the situation with Tim Cohane of *Look Magazine*.

"You probably never heard about a feigned injury until our Iowa game, and I'll tell you why. It's usually the extra seconds gained avail a team little or nothing. Against Iowa, we used the extra seconds to score two touchdowns, a tribute to Notre Dame's typical determination and poise." Leahy went on to explain that it wasn't what was done, but who did it.

Leahy had earlier been involved in the "sucker shift" controversy of 1952. But a 7—2—1 record does not merit the intricate scrutiny of a number one team fighting for its life to maintain an unblemished season ledger.

Other teams utilized the shift and faked injury. But the national coverage that Notre Dame football drew magnified any problem or any success.

Possibly Leahy was too good at what he did: producing winning football teams every year. The cry of "Break up the Irish" could have been yelled after watching most of Frank Leahy's Notre Dame squads.

The Iowa game can best be put in perspective with two revealing comments from employer and employee.

"We shall never de-emphasize the sport as long as I am President of Notre Dame. Frank Leahy is a great credit to this institution." —Fr. Theodore Hesburgh, September 1953.

"Lad, Lad! Leap to your feet and resume the struggle for Our Lady." —Frank Leahy, pre-season practice, 1953.

The struggle continues; Leahy's struggle ended after he battled leukemia, heart trouble and controversy and lost on June 21, 1973. Many believe he was the only one of his kind.

4
MICHIGAN STATE, 1966

"The Ultimate Struggle"

Notre Dame football was in a constant state of flux from 1954 to 1964. While the teams were still supported in the same avid fashion, the unbridled success of Rockne, his coaching pupils and Leahy was not duplicated.

In 1964 the call went to one Ara Raoul Parseghian to lead Notre Dame, and the rest is happy history for the Irish fan. Parseghian instilled confidence, rekindled the "Notre Dame Spirit" and, most importantly, utilized the playing talent to the ultimate. In his first two years under the Dome, Parseghian's teams went 16—3—1. Irish faithful sensed that the Armenian with the coal-black hair and penetrating gaze was a fitting successor to the heritage of former coaching greats.

It is open to question but there are many who believe the Notre Dame football team of 1966 was the most talented group that has ever played for the school. Parseghian and his staff had recruited a team that combined a punishing running attack, potent aerial game and unyielding defense. The molding of this "team of teams" had begun in 1964 by playing some sophomores during the 9—1 season, getting a baptism of fire in 1965 and finding a legendary passing combination during spring practice of 1977.

Spring practice sessions come and go in college football with

Ara and assistant coach Tom Pagna confer on the sidelines.

not much notice. The training gives a coaching staff a chance to look at players who are inexperienced, have served as substitutes or have not played due to injury. Until the freshman eligibility rule was re-introduced, spring practice was a forum for those who had been members of freshman teams and were ready for varsity action. In 1966 spring practice was crucial to Notre Dame because seven new offensive players had to be found before the fall campaign.

Two players from the freshmen team made profound impressions on the college game in the season of 1966. Terry Hanratty, a quarterback with a rocket arm, and Jim Seymour, a rangy wide receiver with great hands, appeared on the cover of *Time Magazine*, made All-America teams and the long bomb an intricate part of the Notre Dame offense.

The defensive unit centered around seniors Jim Lynch and Alan Page. Lynch was the epitome of what the Notre Dame football player should be if central casting made a call. The inside linebacker made Jack Armstrong look like a misfit. His leadership qualities combined with a natural ability to make him a concensus All-American for 1966. Page, who is destined for a position in the NFL Hall of Fame, was a bulwark in the defensive line. At 6'5" and 238 pounds his strength plus speed were matched by few other college athletes.

A close examination of the Notre Dame depth chart of 1966 is staggering. It reads like a who's who of top Irish players by position:

Offense

LE—Jim Seymour, Brian Stenger
LT—Paul Seiler, Fred Schnurr
LG—Tom Regner, Tom McKinley
C—George Goeddeke, Tim Monty
RG—Dick Swatland, Roger

Defense

LE—Tom Rhoads, Allen Sack
LT—Pete Duranko, Harry Alexander
RT—Kevin Hardy, Eric Norri
RE—Alan Page, Chick Lauck
OLB—Mike McGill, John Horney
ILB—Jim Lynch, Ron Jeziorski

Fox
RT—Bob Kuechenberg,
　Rudy Konieczny
RE—Don Gmitter, Mike
　Kuzwicz
QB—Terry Hanratty, Coley
　O'Brien
LH—Nick Eddy, Bob
　Gladieux
RH—Bob Bleier, Frank
　Crniti
FB—Larry Conjar, Paul May

ILB—John Pergine, Ed
　Vuillemin
OLB—Dave Martin, Al
　VanHuffel
LH—Tom O'Leary, Tom
　Quinn
RH—Jim Smithberger, Dan
　Harshman
S—Tom Schoen, Mike
　Burgener

It's doubtful whether any Notre Dame football team has had so many fine players up and down the line, on both offense and defense.

The offensive unit had many weapons to run up the impressive point totals that were accumulated in 1966. Bleier, Eddy and Conjar constituted one of the best backfields in the country, while Hanratty could throw to Seymour, Gmitter or his backs in the multiple-attack game plan.

The best way to describe the defense was "impregnable." The 4-4 alignment refined by linebacker coach John Ray and the other assistants stopped just about every option that was thrown at them. The strong front line, mobile linebackers and quick secondary allowed only thirty-six points in ten games.

Notre Dame swept through its first eight games. Hanratty and Seymour burst onto the national scene as they riddled opposing secondaries for huge chunks of yardage. Their ability to strike for a score from anywhere on the field was a fitting complement to the hard-charging running game of Eddy, Bleier and Conjar.

An opening day twelve-point win over Purdue at Notre Dame Stadium was the closest game the Irish had in their first eight outings. A big test against Oklahoma turned into a romp at Owen Field, as the Sooners were crushed, 38—0.

The team of 1966 was the penultimate juggernaut. It moved with relentless force and brick-walled any attempt by every conceivable offensive formation and game plan.

It is a maxim of successful football teams that while offense may sell tickets, defense wins games. But the Irish units in 1966 were nearly equal in their dominance through the first eight games of the season. The defense gave up but four scores in eight wins while the offense averaged over thirty-seven points.

The confidence both offense and defense built was a natural outgrowth of their success. While always wary of each Saturday opponent, Notre Dame knew it was good in a reasonable, quietly confident way. On November 19, 1977 this confidence had to surface to preserve their unbeaten season and honor.

Michigan State shared the national championship in 1965 with Alabama. Duffy Daugherty had a team that was as powerful as any ever seen in the Big 10. Future pro stars dotted the lineup. George Webster, Clint Jones, Jess Phillips and Bubba Smith were among the best at their respective positions in 1966. The national press knew of the Spartan power. They knew of the Irish power. All eyes turned toward that special Saturday in late November.

Probably no other game in the modern history of college football has been as publicized as Notre Dame—Michigan State of 1966. Either team could have been upset in the games leading to the "big one." If that had happened, Daugherty or Parseghian could have fixed a degree of blame on the undue attention lavished on the Irish-Spartan clash.

It did not happen. The media dream of two untouched, unbowed college football giants meeting head on did occur. But not without tremendously extenuating circumstances.

If the situation were ideal, both squads would lock horns in perfect physical and mental condition. Both would be at their peak for a game that would most likely decide the national championship. The same type of conditions were present at the Notre Dame—Ohio State game of 1935, but neither team grabbed the brass ring; 1966 was different.

The perfect match-up was not to be. Nick Eddy, the powerful and lithe Irish running back, had been nursing a sore shoulder as Notre Dame prepared for the Spartans. He had to be ready to play if the Irish were to have a reasonable shot at MSU.

Notre Dame traveled by train to East Lansing. As the team disembarked at the East Lansing station, Eddy slipped and, as he tried to break his fall, tore the ligaments in his injured shoulder. Eddy's ten touchdowns and 7.1 rushing average could not be utilized in the biggest of big games.

Still, Notre Dame knew they had to give it their all against the Spartans, with or without Eddy. Hanratty and Seymour were ready as were Goedekke, Page, Lynch, Duranko, et al. Before the game few players dreamed that other names would dot the Sunday morning headlines, names that would suddenly jump into national prominence.

The Saturday morning that all had waited for dawned raw, cold and cloudy: a good day for football. The hitting was fierce; defense set the tone of the action.

At the outset the Irish hope to jump on Michigan State and take away the Spartans' emotional advantage and the influence of the home crowd. The quicker a team starts in an away game, the easier it is to settle into the game plan and negate the home team's natural momentum.

Notre Dame gains twenty yards on its first possession. The Irish drive stalls when Bleier loses four on a draw play. A Kevin Hardy punt pins the Spartans on their own 11.

Michigan State can't move and kicks back to the Irish. The next series is one of the most crucial in the game. Hanratty faces second and nine at the MSU 36. He has maneuvered his team into Spartan territory on a twenty-six-yard pass to Bob Gladieux. The Irish have moved into the State end of the field for the second time in the game. The Notre Dame quarterback rolls to his right and runs. But he is hit by Smith and Charlie Thornhill after a two-yard gain.

The tackle by the Green-and-White defenders is crushing. Hanratty's shoulder is separated. He tries unsuccessfully to pass to Bleier. The Irish have now lost a starting running back and quarterback, and the game is not yet a quarter old. But Notre Dame's injury list is just beginning to mount. Before the game ends, Hanratty and Eddy will be joined on the sidelines by Goedekke and Stenger. But in a game with the magnitude of this, neither side will ask for quarter nor give any.

Two widely different emotions could sweep through the teams. Panic was not out of the question for the Irish. Two main offensive weapons are gone, a hostile arena senses the situation, and the opponent is the most formidable in the nation. The Spartans could give in to euphoria. They have Notre Dame reeling. The road has been made easier without Eddy or Hanratty, or so it would seem. But teams destined for national championships maintain an even keel when all else is tilting. Notre Dame remains calm, and Michigan State does not become cocky.

A Michigan State punt gives the ball to the Irish on their own 35. Coley O'Brien is the new quarterback. He is comfortably at home as the leader of the offense. He has waited for his chance, while never being too far behind Hanratty in the opinion of the coaching staff. They would not hesitate to insert O'Brien at any time. But earlier in the season O'Brien was diagnosed as diabetic. His blood-sugar level must be closely maintained. Physical exertion demands even more vigilance. Coley O'Brien is now playing for the number one ranking against the defending national champ. His effort will be remembered for years to come when examples of courage and persistence are recalled.

Hardy's punt gives State the ball on their own 27. Lightning is ready to strike. Jimmy Raye, a slithery quarter-back who is best known for his running, fires a pass for end Gene Washington. Washington has sprinter speed and beats the Irish secondary for a gain of forty-two yards. Washington has a unique way of looking at his opponents as he lines up across the line of scrimmage.

"I can look in a man's eyes and know whether or not I

can beat him," Washington said later. "I knew I could beat those guys all day."

Raye now moves his team to the Notre Dame 20 as the first quarter ends. Regis Cavender at fullback bursts for ten- and five-yard gains, then bolts for the first touchdown of the day from the four yard line. Barefooted Dick Kenney kicks the extra point, and the Spartans hold a seven-point lead.

Notre Dame tries to counter, but a fourteen-yard advance bogs, and Hardy punts again. O'Brien is still adjusting to his new vantage point for the game. He can't afford to take much longer. The State offense is moving.

Raye rips off a thirty-yard gain behind a Clint Jones block, and the crowd is ready for another Spartan score. Dwight Lee rushes for thirteen and the Spartans are in Irish territory. Raye goes to the air for more.

His pass is intercepted by Lynch. As he tries to return the ball, he is turned upside down on the tackle by Jones and loses control of the pigskin. Michigan State has a first down and new life after the play. Lynch's linebacker coach Ray remembers the play:

"Lynch made a fine play. The tackle just flipped him. I could see he was stunned, but he refused to leave. He wanted to make up for it."

Knowing Ray's fiery manner on the sideline, Lynch probably preferred the State blockers and runners to the "suggestions" of John Ray.

Quarterback Raye mixes the pass and run well after the Lynch fumble. He hits Washington for seventeen. The wide receiver is pushed out of bounds by Tom O'Leary to stop the advance. Horney and Duranko stop Cavender after a gain of one and after an illegal motion penalty, Kenney hits a forty-seven-yard field goal. It's 10–0, Michigan State.

The Irish offense is helped out by a fine kickoff return by Tom Quinn for thirty-eight yards out to the 46. O'Brien hits Gladieux for eleven, Bleier for nine, and the ball is at the

Spartan 34. On second-and-one, O'Brien again finds
Gladieux who splits the secondary for the big play and a
thirty-four-yard score. Notre Dame is back in the game after
only four plays following Quinn's return. Joe Azzaro kicks
the extra point, and it's a three-point contest.

"It [the pass] wasn't even intended for him. It was an out
pass for Bleier. Gladieux was the secondary receiver, and I
spotted him as he got behind the secondary," O'Brien later
explained.

The half ends with both defensive units hanging tough.
A three-point lead by State is the margin as the teams head
for intermission instructions from their coaches.

The Notre Dame defense has not played well in the eyes of
coach Ray. "We were good enough not to have allowed
anything. We did not rush well, but our hitting was good.
I felt that we could shut out any team we played and should
have. That's why I was a little upset," Ray recalls. The
defense learns its lesson well and will whitewash the Spartans
in the second half.

Michigan State has outgained the Irish in every category
except passing yardage. The big plays are the Raye pass to
Washington for forty-two yards and the O'Brien connection
to Gladieux for thirty-four yards and the Notre Dame
touchdown.

The second half begins with a big break. On the first play
from scrimmage, Raye fumbles and linebacker Horney
recovers for the Irish on the State 31. The offense goes for
the quick strike after the turnover, but the Spartans are alert
and return the favor. O'Brien tries to hit Bleier out of the
backfield, but Jess Phillips intercepts. Bleier stops the
defensive back on the State two.

Daugherty's offense moves out to the 28, where Kenney
punts to Tom Schoen who makes a fair catch on the Notre
Dame 42. After rushes by Bleier and Conjar, O'Brien sneaks
for a first down at the Spartan 47.

On second-and-seven from the State 44, O'Brien tries to
pass but is sacked by Smith, Chatlos and Richardson. It's a

loss of twelve. A Bleier carry gets five, then Hardy punts to the Spartan five.

For the second straight possession, the Irish defense has the opportunity to keep Michigan State bottled up deep in its own territory. But again it's Jimmy Raye to Gene Washington for the big play. The lithe split receiver falls as he makes the grab at his own 46. It is the last big Spartan offensive play of the afternoon. A nine-yard bolt by Jones puts the ball on the Notre Dame 47, but Pergine nails Bob Apisa for a loss of one. Kenney again has to punt and puts it in the end zone.

O'Brien is beginning to find his niche in the Notre Dame game plan. He hits Bleier for nine and fullback Conjar for eighteen. Coley then finds third string halfback Dave Haley for twenty-three yards to the Spartan 30. Besides the obvious problem presented by Smith, Webster and friends, O'Brien's almost constant motion begins to fatigue him. Still he moves the offense down to the State ten as the third quarter ends. On the last play of the period, O'Brien tries to find a receiver open in the end zone, but Richardson makes the third-down tackle.

On the first play of the last quarter, Joe Azzaro kicks a twenty-eight-yard field goal to pull the Irish even. The Notre Dame scoring march covered fifty-two yards. But the drive has taken a lot out of O'Brien, who immediately heads for the bench after the score. Team doctors try to keep his condition stable.

The Spartan quarterback tries to rejuvenate his team. He sneaks through the onrushing Irish defensive line for twenty to the Notre Dame 46. But a tackle by Hardy Jones for a one-yard loss and another by Lynch for a loss of two on Raye forces a State punt.

The kick carries to the Notre Dame seven. The Irish get the ball out to the 15 where Hardy kicks it back to State. The Spartans have excellent field position at their own 45, but can only move four yards against the defense.

Again the Irish are pinned deep. The ball is on the Notre

Dame 13. Only two yards are gained in the series and Hardy boots a thirty-seven-yard punt. Time is becoming a factor. State has but fifty-two yards between them and a touchdown. After two plays, Raye goes for Lee but is intercepted by Schoen who takes it at midfield and is downed immediately. Schoen is a converted quarterback who has just made the first of two saving plays for the defense down the stretch.

The deadlock is now well into the fourth quarter. O'Brien tries to move the Irish closer to what will probably be the winning score. The Notre Dame defense has taken control of the game. The Spartans have moved at a snail's pace on the ground, and their passing game has begun to sputter.

Notre Dame gains five before Hardy is called on to punt again. It is another amazing fact of this game that Hardy has played on the defensive line and punted for the entire game. His eight kicks for a forty-two-yard average is one of the overlooked outstanding facets of the contest. His last kick of the afternoon is good for forty-five yards and goes into the end zone.

The game has been dominated by defense in the second half. Only quick strikes have broken the trench-like warfare. But on the first Spartan play at the 20, the Irish defenders make their own thunder.

Raye throws for end Allen Brenner, but Schoen again intercepts. He's off for the touchdown but is tackled on the Spartan 18. Irish partisans go wild as they sense the culmination of a great second half effort.

Notre Dame must be cautious with the ball so close to the goal and time winding down. Just over five minutes remain. Earlier in the game the Irish tried to strike immediately after the turnover and lost possession. Conjar gains two but on second-and-eight, Phil Hoag and Smith nail Haley for an eight-yard loss. The Spartan defensive unit has provided its own big play.

O'Brien tries for Seymour, but his pass is deflected, and Azzaro is called on for the field goal attempt. It's a forty-two-yard attempt. He hits it well, but the ball strays and misses by a few feet. State, outplayed in the second half after dominating the first two quarters, breathes a sigh of relief.

The Spartans have the ball for the last time. From the 20 they gain sixteen yards. The MSU defense, on the field for the majority of the third and fourth quarters, is back in action after a punt from their own 36.

Notre Dame now faces a precarious situation. They have come back from a ten-point deficit. They are on the road in front of a hostile stadium. They have been stripped of front-line players by injury. O'Brien's medical status is not good. He is nearly out on his feet. The Irish coaching staff has noticed that his reflexes have slowed, and he shows symptoms of someone slipping into diabetic complications. Parseghian considers sending in Bob Belden at quarterback, but decides against it, not wanting to risk a fumbled handoff.

The fans' wish is plain. They want to see the ball thrown long in hopes of a scoring bomb. Let it fly to Seymour, with all the stops pulled out. But Seymour has been a marked man all day long and has not been much of a factor. He has been blanketed by the Spartan secondary on nearly every route. State's defenders have matched the Irish defense move for move.

Parseghian and his staff opt for the strategy that will draw unbelievable rancor and fire but will prove correct in the long run. One minute and twenty-four seconds remain in the game. State stops three Irish running plays for short gains. On fourth-and-one from his own 39, O'Brien sneaks for a first down. It is interesting to consider the heat Parseghian would have taken if his quarterback had been thrown for a loss or failed to get the first down. A punt is far riskier than a sneak, but that fact has been lost on those who question Notre Dame's play-calling judgment in the last moments of the contest.

O'Brien tries to pass on first-and-ten but is nailed by Smith for a loss of seven. Notre Dame doesn't stop the clock. They allow the remaining seconds to expire and take the tie. The Irish do not risk the comeback from ten points down, nor risk a great performance by a quarterback who probably should not have been in the game. State tries to forestall the inevitable by calling timeouts, but the clock reaches zero, and the game end in a tie.

Notre Dame was unbeaten. So were the Spartans. The inevitable disappointment was apparent on both sides. The absolute perfection that Irish had sought was tainted. The immense pride and self-esteem the entire squad had built was reflected in the despair of the tie. Notre Dame had come back, but that wasn't enough. Winners win; nothing else will do. O'Brien's feelings said it for the team as he sat misty-eyed with his head bowed in front of his locker.

Duffy Daugherty, ever the Hibernian gentleman, told the Notre Dame team not to stumble against Southern California the next week. But he was less than his usual ebullient self with the press. He emphasized he was going for the win on fourth-and-one from his own 29 with time running out. Daugherty's players were livid with the final few moments of the game.

"We couldn't believe it," said Webster. "We were really stunned. Then it dawned on us. They were playing for the tie."

"The tie didn't prove a damn thing. All it does is make you wonder. We wanted to find out who was better," said Bubba Smith.

Parseghian knew he would have to explain his actions. He did with logic and conviction to the assembled press corps.

"I wasn't going to blow the game with an interception. The decision [to take the tie] also was made in deference to Dick Kenney's field goal ability.

"The way our kids fought back from that 10-to-0 deficit—I'm proud of them," said the Irish coach. "I didn't realize it at the time, but we had five sophomores in our offensive lineup. It was a rough thing to have those kids go out so early."

Coley O'Brien was the star of the Irish effort. He accepted his role but was somewhat reserved about its effect. "I wasn't all that nervous, although I guess I should have been."

On the late game conservatism O'Brien echoed his coach's sentiments. "They played a prevent defense, and we decided to run the ball."

Game statistics are interesting but do not reflect the vicious contact on both sides of the line. Raye led the State rushers with seventy-five net yards while Bleier had fifty-three for Notre Dame. Lynch had thirteen tackles to pace the Irish while Thornhill had sixteen for the Spartans.

Two differing opinions on the game were provided by a pair of prestigious sportswriters in attendance—Dan Jenkins of *Sports Illustrated* and Joe Falls of the *Detroit Free Press*. Jenkins took the Irish to task for the last-minute strategy.

"A No. 1 team will try something, won't it, to stay that way? Notre Dame did not. It just let the air out of the ball. For reasons that it will rationalize as being more valid than they perhaps were under the immense circumstances, the Irish rode out the clock."

Falls, who has been known to write articles less than favorable in the eyes of Irish fans, saw the big game differently.

"It was regrettable that the game ended in a chorus of boos from the highly partisan crowd as Ara Parseghian chose to settle for the tie instead of trying for a bolt of lightning in the last minute. It would have been far better to see the Irish making an all-out effort to break the tie. But there is a time to gamble, and there isn't a time to gamble. This wasn't the time."

Notre Dame demolished USC in the final game, 51—0. State could not return to the Rose Bowl and had to settle for a tie on their unbeaten record. One wire service voted Michigan State the national champ, while the other selected Notre Dame. Neither team was satisfied with the outcome of the game of November 19, 1966. Surely the co-national championships appeased the players and coaches to a certain degree, yet it would be quite a while before Parseghian's strategy would be justified in the eyes of many. But for his team, and the team's fans, the decisions were never doubted. What others thought did not matter that much anyway.

5

USC, 1970

"Trojans, Torrents, and Theismann"

Should any Notre Dame team ever be so unfortunate as to post a 1—10 season, there is little doubt that most fans would want the lone victory to be over the University of Southern California.

No other team has played the Irish tougher over the entire history of Notre Dame football than USC. Going into the 1981 season, the record favored the Irish with twenty-seven wins, twenty-one losses and four ties. Each game in the series has been a mighty battle between teams that have the highest regard for one another.

The series began in 1926 with Notre Dame winning 13—12 in Los Angeles. The longest winning streak for either team consisted of the five wins recorded by the Irish from 1940—47 (no games were played in '43, '44 and '45) and 1957—61. Some of the greatest names in college football history have participated in the rivalry. For both the Irish and the Trojans, the game has become the most important during the regular season. For many years Army was Notre Dame's "big name" opponent, but after 1946, USC became the major rival.

It has been common in the games between USC and Notre Dame that the team that was supposed to win, did not. A sure victory often has been lost on one crucial play.

The one ongoing characteristic of the rivalry has been the high quality of players each team has fielded. Even when an Irish or Trojan team has been down, the lesser squad nearly always has given a great effort that lends more charisma to the series.

Since 1966, Notre Dame has won only three times (in '72, '74 and '78), but each of the three wins was part of a national championship season for the Irish.

After the crushing 51–0 Irish victory in 1966, USC coach John McKay vowed he would never, ever be beaten like that again. Beating Notre Dame became a personal crusade for the white-haired coach. The Pac 8 title, with its Rose Bowl bid, was very important to McKay, but a win over Notre Dame was a special victory to be savored.

For the next few years after 1966, McKay made good on his promise. In 1967, the Trojans won 24–7 at Notre Dame Stadium, while in 1968 and '69 the games ended in ties. Both teams had ample opportunities to win each year, but missed chances left the games deadlocked.

The passing combination of Hanratty and Seymour, which propelled Notre Dame to national honors in 1966, rewrote the Irish record book in 1967 and 1968. Notre Dame compiled a record of 15–4–1 in the two seasons. Two losses to Purdue, one to USC and one to Michigan State were the only blemishes on the two-year record.

But even the best college teams don't last forever, and Ara Parseghian and his staff had to begin rebuilding the squad. New names and faces replaced the Lynches, Gladieuxes, Pages, Schoens and Eddys. The players who succeeded them were the likes of DiNardo, Gatewood, Patulski, Gulyas and Theismann.

The rebuilding peaked in 1970. The 101st year of college football was important for Notre Dame. The Irish broke with a forty-five-year tradition of not accepting a bowl bid. They lost 21–17 to number-one ranked Texas in the 1970 Cotton Bowl. But keen observers of the college game realized the next Irish squad would have national championship potential.

At the center of the fine team of 1970 was Joe Theismann.

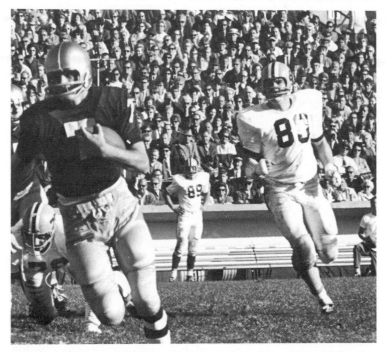

Equally dangerous running or passing, Theismann takes off for daylight.

It is true that his last name originally was pronounced with a long *e*, but Joe altered the pronunciation so that the long *e* became a long *i* as in *Heisman*.

A tremendously gifted athlete, Theismann could run and pass with nearly equal effectiveness. On the dead run, he could pull up and fire a bullet downfield to a wide-open receiver. He was dangerous from any point on the field. But more importantly Theismann possessed the perfect mental attitude for a quarterback. He was quietly confident with an understated cockiness.

The 1970 Notre Dame team ripped through the first part of its schedule as if it had something to prove. The Irish scored points rapidly, and the defense was as good as any in the country.

Notre Dame had no great running back that year, but

Theismann quiets the Notre Dame crowd as he leads the Irish toward another score.

Denny Allan, Bill Barz and Gulyas along with Bob Minnix, Larry Parker and Darryl Dewan were perfect for the multiple offense that revolved around Theismann. He constantly put pressure on the defensive flanks with run-pass options. Theismann could drop back and throw to Tom Gatewood and tight end Mike Creaney or simply tuck the ball and take off while the defense tried to hem him in.

Walt Patulski, Mike Kadish, Greg Marx, Tim Kelly and Clarence Ellis were the leaders of the defense that held foes to fifty-nine points through the first nine games.

Traditionally a Notre Dame home game against USC comes at mid-season. So it's often quite chilly for the visitors. When the Trojans are the home team, the game is always the last of the season, and the weather is usually balmy.

South Bend's climate puts the Irish at a disadvantage in the annual contest, especially when the game is played in Los Angeles. While inclement weather in South Bend often prevents outside practice by the Irish, the Trojans have no such problem.

The home game belonged to USC in 1970. The two teams came into the annual battle with two very different seasonal paths. The Irish already had accepted a Cotton Bowl bid for a return visit to Dallas to face Texas and had a shot at the national championship. USC was finishing a disappointing season.

The oddsmakers favored Notre Dame, with good reason. Notre Dame would field its best team since 1977 against USC on November 28, 1970. Parseghian's team was rated third in the country, while the Trojans were, at best, a team in a slump. McKay characterized his squad's 45—20 loss to UCLA as "the worst defensive game any team of mine has ever played."

But the two rivals had a third foe with which to contend. Dull and overcast skies greeted the squads as they went through their warm-up routines. The postcard-perfect sunny weather that is usually found in Los Angeles was nowhere around. First it began to drizzle lightly, but by the time the game had moved into the third quarter, the drizzle was a downpour and the field was a mudhole.

After winning the toss, the Irish offense goes to work. Theismann has the hot hand and bets heavy. He finds Gatewood for nineteen and Cieszkowski for twelve; he runs for four, throws to Dewan and then gives to Gulyas for three, and it's a first down on the Trojan 28. The Irish quarterback then keeps the ball over left tackle. He breaks clear at the line of scrimmage and threads his way through the USC secondary. Four minutes and seven seconds have been played in the first quarter as Theismann goes in for six points. Scott Hempel kicks the extra point, and the score is 7—0, Irish.

The rain is now coming down harder. But it doesn't stop the Men of Troy. Clarence Davis, Sam Cunningham and Jimmy Jones are the offensive weapons as USC marches down the field to tie the game at seven. Nearly seven minutes have been played. The tone of the game has been set: Points will be rung up with great frequency and the rain will be relentless.

The next Irish offensive series starts with a sack of Theismann by Willie Hall that loses eight yards. The Irish can't make a first down, so Jim Yoder punts to the Trojans. And quarterback Jones goes to work. He hits Davis with a thirty-one-yard pass that takes the ball down to the Notre Dame 18. Jones hits Bob Chandler for ten and Davis bolts in for the score from five yards out. Ron Ayala misses the conversion and it's 13–7, USC.

After three plays, Notre Dame must punt again. USC has the ball on its own 43. Jones is back to throw but slips in the mud for a loss of seven. He then comes right back to Davis on a screen for a gain of ten. After a nine-yard pass to Evans, Jones hurls the bomb to speedster Sam Dickerson.

The rush of ends Bob Neidert and Walt Patulski has been pushed back for most of the first quarter. Again the protection holds as Dickerson runs for the ball. The forty-five-yard pass goes off Clarence Ellis' shoulder and into the receiver's hands for the touchdown. The first period hasn't ended and USC already has its third score. A two-point conversion from Jones to Chandler is good, and it's 21–7, Trojans.

The Irish must rebound and the quicker the better. USC is thinking upset. Theismann finds Gulyas for twenty-six, but Notre Dame is penalized for a clip. The first quarter finally ends with USC holding a fourteen-point lead. The rain is now a downpour.

Theismann finds Creaney for a nineteen-yard gain, but the tight end fumbles and the Trojans recover. The Irish defense holds and forces the first USC punt of the day. The offense can't move, and Yoder kicks it back.

Again it is Jones to Dickerson for the big gain. The twenty-seven-yard connection takes the ball to midfield where Notre Dame's defense stiffens. Neidert nabs Rod McNeill for a nine-yard loss on third-and-eight, and Ayala is forced to kick. Each punt is a costly maneuver with the weather deteriorating by the minute.

Theismann opens up the passing lanes and hits Gatewood for a twenty-eight-yard pickup. A personal foul penalty against USC puts the ball on the Trojan 24. Two incompletions make it third-and-ten as Theismann hits Dewan for fourteen. The Irish score a second time as Cieszkowski takes the swing pass and leaps over for the touchdown from the two-yard line. Hempel converts, and Notre Dame is within seven at 21—14 with 7:24 showing on the clock in the first half.

The Trojans can't advance after taking the kickoff but Theismann is intercepted by Dyer at the Notre Dame 47. USC relentlessly takes the ball downfield. The Irish defense puts up a great stand, holding the Trojans four times inside the five before Ayala hits the field goal from the nine, and USC goes up by ten, 24–14.

Momentum is the object that the Irish hope to grasp. Theismann rolls, throws, runs and squirms his way upfield despite the slop and muddy conditions. The quarterback is playing the clock well. He has twenty-one seconds left in the half as he finds Creaney for a gain of twenty-one. He goes to Gatewood for six with eleven seconds showing. The Irish now have the ball in Trojan territory. Gatewood takes another out pass for a seven-yard gain that stops the clock with eight seconds left. The ball is at the 32 as Hempel comes on the field to attempt a forty-nine-yard field goal. But the kick is short, and the Trojans hold onto the ten-point lead at halftime.

The Notre Dame defense has rallied after surrendering three touchdowns by holding USC to the Ayala field goal. The Irish offense has moved the ball well despite the worsening weather. The ten-point lead does not seem much to overcome for a team that has not been defeated in nine games.

Theismann has already passed for enough yardage to please most college quarterbacks for an entire afternoon. His 219 yards have come on fifteen completions. His counterpart Jones has found the range for 189 yards on eleven successful attempts. Clarence Davis has a fine day going as he has rushed for seventy-two yards on seventeen carries. Theismann is the leading Irish ball carrier with thirty-seven yards on six carries. The game is still up for grabs as the rain continues to pelt the fans who have decided to wait out the unusual weather. Little did any know that more than rain would tumble down in the third quarter.

After giving up one first down, the Irish defense forces a Trojan punt. The ball hits dead on the Notre Dame 19, where Theismann and his offense set up shop.

The quarterback hands off to Dewan who fumbles. Kent Carter recovers for USC, and the tide turns irrevocably to the Garnet and Gold.

Jimmy Jones takes only four plays to get the touchdown, but the score comes after running-back Mike Berry fumbles into the end zone. The ball is free for either Notre Dame or USC to recover. An Irish possession would give the ball back to the offense on the 20, but tackle Sam Adams is there for the Trojans, and he smothers the ball for the six-pointer. Ayala converts, and it's USC leading a shocked Notre Dame, 31—14.

The "fumbleitis" continues for the Irish as Bob Minnix can't hold on after taking the kickoff. Luckily for the visitors Bill Trapp recovers. Dame Fortune has decided not to gaze on Parseghian's team. On the first play from scrimmage, Theismann fumbles, recovers and is dumped for a loss of eleven. He tries to pass from the end zone on the next play and fumbles again. The hit by Hall sets the ball bounding free in the end zone where John Vella takes possession for another Trojan score. The Irish are finding out that even a 5—4—1 team is hard to handle when given the opportunities that USC has had. Ayala's kick makes it 38—14, Trojans.

A mere forty-two seconds have pushed McKay's team from ten points ahead to 24. The lead is insurmountable, but no one has told Notre Dame and especially Joe Theismann.

The Trojan fans are taken aback with the turn of events. Their team that was trounced by UCLA has the third best squad in the country on the run. What began as a potentially interesting game between a favored team and a weak traditional rival is quickly becoming a rout.

When all seems to be heading into the drains of the Coliseum (along with most of the field), the Irish begin fighting back in true Notre Dame style.

The effort centers on Theismann. After getting the ball on his own 28, he moves the team ten yards upfield. He then hits Larry Parker for ten more, Parker runs for four and Theismann then hits Parker for a forty-six-yard bomb. Parker has beaten his man and takes it into the end zone for a score. He outran the defender from the 25, and when Hempel converts it's 38–21, USC.

After the scoring barrage at the beginning of the quarter, punts become the order of the day for the next few series. The quarter winds down as the Notre Dame offense is moving again. From the Irish 31, Theismann takes the team toward the USC goal. As the rain comes down in sheets, Creaney, Cieszkowski and Gulyas all catch Theismann passes for gains. Even Joe makes a reception when Vella blocks a pass back into the quarterback's hands. Theismann gains seven yards with the catch. The quarter ends with Notre Dame at the USC five yard line with second-and-goal.

Three plays into the final period, Theismann takes it over, and it's 38–28, USC. The seemingly insurmountable lead suddenly is shrinking.

The Irish have a chance to make the big turnaround play when the kickoff is fumbled, but the Trojans recapture the ball. The defense stops any movement upfield, and Ayala punts to Ellis who makes the fair catch at the Notre Dame 37.

The Trojan defense now knows that Theismann must throw. The rush is full tilt. Hall once again nails Theismann for a loss, this one for ten yards. On third-and-twenty, Parker grabs a sixteen-yard toss, but Yoder is called on to punt on fourth down.

USC tries to milk time off the clock with its running game, but Notre Dame's defense digs in. The ball goes back to the Irish as the clock winds down in the final quarter.

Another drive begins. Theismann hits Gatewood for nine, Parker latches onto a flat pass and skirts through the defense for a fifty-six yard gain. The ball is down to the Trojan 25. Notre Dame fans who have made the cross-country journey know that they are witnessing a truly memorable performance and with that knowledge, hope rises that Theismann will complete his crusade successfully. But Hall is again in on Joe and sacks him for an eleven-yard loss. The ball goes back to the Trojan 36 as Yoder shanks a punt for only nine yards.

Ayala returns the favor and Notre Dame has the ball on its own 49. Theismann is intercepted by Carter, who takes it back to the Irish 37. But there is no movement as the Trojan offense can't make any headway and Notre Dame gets the ball back on the nine.

All on passes, it's Gatewood for twenty, Parker for sixteen and ten, Barz for seven and Gatewood again for thirteen. But time is running out as Theismann tries in vain to keep the Irish unbeaten. With first-and-ten on the USC 25, the Trojans intercept to stop the drive.

A dejected Theismann gestures to the sidelines, knowing the game is over. He strikes a pleading gesture amid the sea of mud. His white no. 7 jersey is splattered with the remnants of an afternoon that he will never forget. In his last regular season game for Notre Dame, he is the picture of frustration. A photo taken at this moment later was captioned: "What more can one man do for Notre Dame?" The final score is 38–28.

The two quick scores at the beginning of the third quarter were the difference. But Theismann's incredible effort is best reflected in the stats: Thirty-three completions, fifty-eight attempts, four interceptions and two touchdowns. Two rushing scores were combined with his passing marks. It totaled 526 yards. The most hardened Irish-hater must admit the incredible occurred on November 28, 1970.

The "other quarterback" also had a fine game. Jimmy Jones played the best sixty minutes of his career in guiding the upset. He was fifteen of twenty-four through the air for 226 yards.

"We showed what kind of team we are. Everybody was relaxed and wanted to play football. We really put it all together," said Jones.

John McKay had done it again. He had beaten Notre Dame and had cost the Irish dearly. But the veteran coach was gracious in victory.

"Don't take anything away from Notre Dame. They are a great team. Theismann did a great job of throwing. By the way he's a good one." McKay's penchant for understatement never knew a keener moment.

"It doesn't make any difference whether you lose by one or forty points. . . . Yes, the rain hurt us because it's hard to play catch-up football when you can't even keep your footing," responded Parseghian when asked about his team's only loss of the year.

The individual statistics meant nothing to Theismann. He concentrated on his mistakes.

"I made the big one, that fumble in the end zone. That cost us the ballgame. But I have no excuses. They beat us; they beat us bad." Theismann's words sounded like shouts in the silent locker room as he talked with Jack Tobin of *Sports Illustrated*.

Notre Dame rebounded from the disaster in the mud. Taking on top-ranked Texas in the Cotton Bowl, the Irish won 24–11 and cost the Horns their second straight national title. Nebraska was named the top team, and Jim Plunkett won the Heisman Trophy. The balloting was completed before November 28. Joe Theismann was second.

6

ALABAMA, 1973

"The Sweetest"

The Parseghian years at Notre Dame were replete with great performances by teams and individuals. From 1964 to 1974, the Irish were nearly always a top-ten team and a candidate for national honors. Following Notre Dame's first bowl win in forty-six years, the 1971 team logged an 8—2 season. The squad was in line for a bowl game bid, probably against Penn State in the Gator Bowl. Yet the team decided not to accept a bid. Rumors concerning the refusal made the rounds, but in retrospect it was probably best that the Irish stayed home. A team that does not want to play in a bowl game usually is destined for a long afternoon.

The 1972 season saw improvement. An upset loss to Missouri in mid-season still provokes heated discussions among faithful fans. The crucial Tiger score came when Don Johnson dropped the ball after taking the handoff close to the Irish goal. The referee signaled a touchdown despite protests from the defensive unit and the coaching staff. The call stood, and Mizzou won the game by a 30—26 score. USC made it three in a row over the Irish later in the year with a 45—23 trouncing in Los Angeles. Sophomore Anthony Davis tallied six touchdowns in an afternoon in which he danced on his knees following a score.

Notre Dame accepted a bid to the Orange Bowl and suffered its second straight embarrassing loss when Nebraska, the eventual national champion, defeated the Irish, 40—6.

After the loss in Miami, Parseghian and his staff hit the recruiting trail with a vengeance. The result was a freshman class in 1973 among the best to arrive on campus. Ross Browner, Willie Fry, Al Hunter, Dan Kelleher and Jim Weiler were but a few of the first-year players in 1973. This class coupled with the previous year's recruiting crop (Niehaus, Stock, Best, etc.) gave the Irish a fine collection of underclassmen.

The juniors and seniors were also a talented aggregation. A fine quarterback returned in Tom Clements. He had two talented receivers in Pete Demmerle and Dave Casper (who was moved to tight end from off tackle). The offensive line was solid with Steve Neece, Frank Pomarico, Mark Brenneman, Gerry DiNardo and Steve Sylvester. Eric Penick and Wayne Bullock were in the offensive backfield. The defense was led by tackle Mike Fanning, linebackers Gary Potempa, Greg Collins and Drew Mahalic. Mike Townsend and Reggie Barnett keyed the secondary.

Parseghian used a fine psychological tool during the summer hiatus. He sent each player a letter noting the Irish success over the previous five years and the errors and shortcomings that had plunged them to defeat in the Orange Bowl. He wrote the message in a controlled and business-like fashion that reinstilled confidence and alerted the players to the problems that could occur if the highest degree of intensity were not maintained.

The Irish of 1973 had everything needed for a championship squad. They had a good kicking game and a perfect blend of veteran and young talent which gave the team depth.

Tom Clements led Notre Dame to sixty-four points in the first two games. He did not possess the physical talents of Theismann, but his leadership qualities were unsurpassed. Clements was a threat running or passing, but his best asset was his avoidance of the big mistake. With Casper and

Demmerle receiving, Clements could use his superb ball handling and faking to augment the running game.

The closest game on the early part of the schedule was the 14—10 win over Michigan State. But the biggest hurdle of the regular season was the October battle with USC.

"Revenge" was the watchword in preparing for the Trojans. Anthony Davis was a marked man stymied all day. The tone of the game was set early when freshman Bradley knocked Lynn Swann from the ball, his helmet and his senses on an attempted screen pass. Penick's eighty-five-yard-run early in the third quarter was the clincher as Notre Dame won, 23—14. Wins over Navy, Pitt, Air Force and Miami gave Notre Dame a 10—0 mark for the regular season.

The Irish were invited to play Alabama in the Sugar Bowl on New Year's Eve. Tulane Stadium was the site for the game to decide the national championship.

The Crimson Tide had had a great year. They led the country in scoring and offensive yardage. Bear Bryant used the wishbone offense as a steamrolling machine with quarterbacks Gary Rutledge and Richard Todd handing off to running backs Mike Stock, Wilbur Jackson, Randy Billingsley and Willie Shelby. The defense was a swarming bunch with end Leroy Cook, linebacker Woody Lowe and defensive back Mike Washington having few peers across the country.

The Sugar Bowl is a difficult game to prepare for. The fantastic sights and sounds of nighttime New Orleans are enough to distract the most dedicated athlete. Bourbon Street after dark is a tempting invitation for any visitor, whether a conventioneer or a college football player. But both squads understood the game's significance, and knuckled down for tough practices.

Much anticipation surrounded this first meeting between two schools long associated with football success. Two great coaches met at midfield for the first time, Parseghian and Bear Bryant.

Rain fell in New Orleans for most of the week and for most of December 31. But the downpour slacked just before game

time. The artificial turf had a thin layer of water on the surface as the game began.

Most observers favored 'Bama because of its tremendous
offensive power. Alabama's speed and size were almost impossible to defend against. Notre Dame employed the "mirror
defense" to try and stop the wishbone. Parseghian and his
staff invented it for the second Cotton Bowl with Texas, and
the strategy had been a key to the 24—11 Irish victory. But
Texas did not have the Tide's talent at quarterback. Todd
and Rutledge often alternated during a game with little re-
duction in effectiveness. Alabama's passing game was also
much better than most wishbone offenses.

A calm wind and 55° temperatures were the weather read-
ings at kickoff. Tulane Stadium rocked with shouts of "Roll
Tide" and "Go Irish."

Notre Dame wins the toss, and Gary Diminick takes the
boot in the end zone for a touchback. Bullock gains twenty
yards on two carries before Clements loses a yard at the Notre
Dame 43. Bullock then gets six and ten yards on runs that take
the ball to midfield. The drive stalls on the Alabama 39 and
Brian Doherty punts dead at the sixteen.

The Tide must punt after three plays. Greg Gantt kicks to
Bob Zanot and the Irish have the ball on its 40. Best gets four
and Penick three, but David McMakin stops Penick on third
down for no gain. Doherty punts back to 'Bama.

Time runs out in the first quarter as Gantt kicks again to
Zanot after the Tide is stopped. Notre Dame has the ball on
its own 36. The kick carries forty-four yards. Clements comes
out throwing and finds Demmerle for nineteen. He again
hooks up with the split end for a twenty-six-yard gain on
second-and-seven that takes the ball to the 'Bama seventeen.
It's Clements to Demmerle again for fourteen yards as the
All-America receiver puts the ball on the Tide three. The Irish
punch the ball over in three plays with Bullock scoring from
the one. The snap on the conversion is fumbled and the Irish
lead, 6–0, with 2:32 left on the clock in the first period.

Wayne Bullock carries into the Crimson Tide line after taking the handoff from quarterback Tom Clements. Bullock scored the first touchdown of the game giving the Irish a 6-0 lead.

The Notre Dame offense spread out the 'Bama defenders on the scoring drive. The Irish discovered they could throw against the Tide's 5–2 defensive alignment, and Clements picked out the seams in the coverage. The drive covered sixty-four yards in but seven plays.

After Alabama takes the kickoff, defensive end Browner makes the big play. On third-and-five, Browner breaks through the line to sack Rutledge. Gantt punts out of bounds a yard inside midfield at the Tide 49. Notre Dame moves the ball to the 46 but is forced to punt as the first quarter ends with the Irish ahead, 6–0.

Alabama fires up its offense by using the pass. Rutledge hits George Pugh for fifteen and Paul Spivey for ten. From the Tide 45, Billingsley gains sixteen before safety Bradley makes the stop. But the drive dies suddenly at the Notre Dame seventeen as Rutledge fumbles, and Jim Stock recovers. However, Bullock coughs the ball up at the Irish 46, and 'Bama begins to move again.

From the Tide 48, Rutledge uses only seven plays to gain the equalizer. Billingsley takes the ball into the end zone from the Notre Dame six at the halfway point of the second quarter. Bill Davis kicks the extra point and it's a one point lead for Bryant's team.

The second quarter has been all Alabama. The wishbone offense is moving well and Rutledge has his backs gaining the yardage in big chunks inside and outside. The Irish need a big play to arrest the 'Bama momentum.

It comes immediately. Al Hunter takes Gantt's kickoff at his own seven. The man who eventually gained more than 1,000 yards in a single season does not break stride once after hitting full speed. Hunter streaks into the end zone with a 93–yard run. It's the longest return in Sugar Bowl history. The play that sprung Hunter has been practiced on in pre-game workouts, and it worked perfectly. Clements finds Demmerle for the two-point conversion, and Notre Dame is back on top, 14–7, with 7:07 remaining in the half.

Both teams punt after failing to gain first downs; 3:18 is left in the quarter as Rutledge hits Pugh for a gain of fourteen out to the Tide 32. Following a time out, Jackson runs for twenty-one around right end. At the Notre Dame 29, Jackson gets six more to the 23. On third-and-four, Mahalic stops Jackson on the 22 after the Tide back takes a Rutledge swing pass. Davis comes on to hit a thirty-nine-yard field goal, and it's a 14–10 game. Notre Dame moves the ball after the kickoff to the 'Bama 31 following a pass-interference call. Bob Thomas misfires on a 48-yard field-goal attempt, and the Irish take a four-point lead to the locker room.

The halftime stats reflect the closeness of the game. Notre Dame has a thirty-one-yard lead in total offense but only twenty seconds separate the teams in possession time. Coach Bryant has made one very important strategic move during the half. Utilizing fine depth, Alabama played sixty men in

the first two quarters. Anticipating a battle to the end,
Bryant wants as many fresh players as possible down the
stretch.

The second half is almost a carbon copy of Alabama's
thrust in the second quarter. Eroding both time and yardage,
Rutledge advances his team upfield. A personal foul against
Tim Rudnick puts the ball into Irish territory at the Notre
Dame 42. Switching gears, Rutledge finds Jackson through the
air for a twenty-one-yard pickup to the eighteen. Rutledge
throws again for more real estate, hitting Wayne Wheeler for
thirteen. On the next play Jackson scores from the five.
Davis' kick is true, and 'Bama is back in the lead, 17—14,
with just over eleven minutes left in the quarter.

Notre Dame trails for the second time in the game. The
offense is pinned down on its own ten and Doherty punts the
ball well out to midfield.

Richard Todd is in the game at quarterback for the Tide.
The future New York Jet takes his team down to the Irish
28, where Davis' field goal attempt is wide to the right. With
6:49 remaining in the quarter, Notre Dame starts a drive that
is highlighted by a twenty-seven-yard completion from
Clements to Casper. The Tide defense digs in, and Thomas
misses a fifty-four-yard field goal.

Alabama has the ball on the 20, and again the Irish make
the big play. On third-and-nine from the 21, Willie Shelby
fumbles, linebacker Mahalic grabs the ball while it's still in
the air and gets eight yards before being tackled. The ball is
on the Tide twelve as Notre Dame looks to pull ahead.

They waste no time as Bullock rambles for the touchdown
with Casper taking out defenders on two great blocks. The
Irish are now up 21—17, as Thomas converts. The quarter
ends with Notre Dame getting the ball back. The slippery
turf is becoming more of a factor in the game. Both teams
are having trouble holding onto the eel-like ball. The turnover bug hits the Irish, as Best fumbles at the Tide 25. He
had gained fourteen but on the next play dropped the ball and
McMakin recovered.

'Bama makes a first down as the turnovers continue. Barnett intercepts a Rutledge pass and Notre Dame has possession back on its own 32. Again the ball goes back when Bullock mishandles the pigskin, and the Tide reccvers.

There is no denying 'Bama this time. From the point of the turnover, four plays gain twelve. Todd comes back into the game on third-and-seven at the Notre Dame 25. The Irish try to prevent the first down with a blitz. They play right into Bryant's hands, as Todd gives to Mike Stock who turns and dumps the ball to Todd in the flat. The quarterback takes it into the end zone behind the befuddled defense. Nine minutes and thirty-three seconds remain in the game. But as with the first touchdown, the last touchdown is followed by a missed conversion. The snap is high, and 'Bama settles for a two-point lead, 23—21.

Notre Dame is in a pinch and certainly cannot afford to panic. The Irish must move the ball, or an undefeated season is but a dream. The offense can't afford to turn the ball back to Alabama since the wishbone is a great ball-control offense. Diminick takes the kickoff and returns it to the 19.

Hunter gets the Irish better field possession as he picks up fifteen off tackle. Penick gets four and Clements runs for eight. It's first down at the Notre Dame 46. Bullock fails to gain, but Clements comes back for a nine-yard advance. It is third-and-one; Clements goes for the bomb to his tight end. Casper "The Ghost" is covered but leaps high to outgrab the Tide defenders. Suddenly the ball is at the 'Bama fifteen. The completion is worth thirty yards.

Moving cautiously, Notre Dame gets the ball down to the 'Bama two-yard line, where on fourth down Thomas is called on to kick the tension-packed field goal. Doherty is the holder. The nineteen-yard effort wobbles, wiggles and squirms inside the right goal post. Thomas' contact with the ball is marginal at best, but the Irish have the lead again at 24—23. It is to be the last score of the evening, but the excitement is far from over. Four minutes and twelve seconds remain in the game.

Alabama's offense gains nothing, and Gantt must punt. He booms a sixty-nine yarder, but Browner is called for roughing the kicker. On the offensive series, the Tide has lost eight yards. The fifteen on the penalty will not give 'Bama a first down. Gantt's kick is dead at the Notre Dame one-yard line. Bryant declines the penalty.

There are three minutes left to play. The Irish must gain a first down or face punting from its own end zone. Even if Doherty matches his best kick of the night, the Tide will have excellent field position to move in for the winning points.

Bullock hammers for four, then gets one. It's third-and-six from the five-yard line. Clements calls time-out and goes to the sideline to confer with Parseghian and backfield-coach Tom Pagna. Seven years of criticism and second guessing is about to end for Ara Parseghian. Pagna relates the discussion in his book with Bob Best, *The Era of Ara*.

"I know it's risky, but let's go with a long cadence," suggested Pagna.

Parseghian agreed, then shocked both his assistant and quarterback.

"Tom, take a long count and set up a run-action pass to Casper," instructed Ara.

But the play doesn't materialize. In a two-tight-end set, Casper jumps the snap count, and the ball goes back to the two-yard line. With 2:12 on the clock, Parseghian signals for the same play. The other tight end in the alignment is Robin Weber. He has never caught a pass in a game for Notre Dame.

The 'Bama defense keys on Casper as the ball is snapped. Clements faces right then looks back to the left. Defensive end Cook leaps high getting ready to sack the quarterback when Clements fires the ball to Weber. He grabs it, juggles it and then goes down. It's a thirty-five-yard gain and as gutsy a call as ever made in college football.

The remainder of the time is gobbled up on six plays. Clements falls on the ball at his own 49 as the game ends. Parseghian is carried off the field by his joyous team. The

The catch. Robin Weber takes in a Clements toss to assure the Irish the 1973 national title. Weber hung on despite bobbling the ball. Bear Bryant and his team look on helplessly as the 24-23 win is locked up.

Alabama players, pictures of dejection and envy, are full of class as they congratulate the victors. Parseghian is besieged by reporters in the locker room.

"The pass from Clements to Weber was the key to the win," Parseghian said after the game. "If we didn't make the first down, Alabama would surely have been in field goal position with us punting from our end zone."

Parseghian complimented Alabama on its effort. "I definitely feel we're the national champs. We beat the leading scoring team in the nation and the team that was leading in offensive yardage. They are an excellently disciplined team. We beat a great football team, and they lost to a great football team."

Bryant was the epitome of the southern gentleman following the game. He went to the locker room to congratulate Notre Dame and then commented on the razor-thin loss.

"I don't really feel like we lost, just that time ran out on us. Notre Dame came up with a lot of big plays. Ara and his staff did a fine job of preparing for us. They all played well. Tom Clements and their big tight end [Casper] beat us. They didn't do anything new defensively. . . . I think Notre Dame is a great team, but I wouldn't mind playing them again tomorrow. In fact I'd like it."

Irish assistant coach Greg Blache was near Parseghian when the crucial call was made with 2:12 left. "The defense went with the motion of the backfield. They were all looking for Casper. Ara was always at least one play ahead of everybody, and he knew it would work."

Clements was named the MVP for the game. The junior

It wasn't the best kick of his career but Bob Thomas got the 19-yarder to wobble through the uprights to beat Alabama in the 1973 Sugar Bowl.

quarterback gained seventy-four yards on fifteen carries and passed for 169 yards in hitting seven out of twelve passes.

The winning points on Thomas' field goal that slithered through the goal posts provoked this comment from the kicker:

"I was thinking on the way out that if I stuck it right down the pipe nobody would remember it. This way they'll be talking about it for years."

Seven-and-a-half years after the final gun had sounded, Parseghian talked about the pass to Weber.

"I'd do it again in a second. We had no choice. I've received far too much credit for that call and too much criticism for the Michigan State game in 1966. . . . It's just one of those things you have to do at the time."

The Parseghian years at Notre Dame ended in 1975 after a 9—2 season in 1974 that taxed the coach physically and emotionally. He left Notre Dame as he had come: a winner in every aspect. His final victory, giving the '74 Irish a 10—2 record, was foreshadowed on December 31, 1973. The previous shoulder ride Ara Parseghian had off a field was on that day after the 13—11 Orange Bowl win over Alabama. The Sugar Bowl victory was a fitting end for one of the most exciting and successful of Notre Dame coaches.

7

AIR FORCE, 1975

"Rollin' in the Rockies"

When the Irish took the field against Boston College in the first game of 1975 the head coach was Dan Devine. The choice of Devine to succeed the immensely popular Ara Parseghian as the 23rd Notre Dame head football coach took many people by surprise.

Almost immediately following the announcement that Devine would take over, many fans began to grumble. Devine was almost the exact opposite of Parseghian. This added to the hard times Devine had endured while coaching the Green Bay Packers and left Devine with problems before the season kicked off.

But a football program with Notre Dame's heritage does not fail because of innuendo and rumor. Two of the main reasons that Devine succeeded in his first year, despite nearly constant reports of discord, were excellent recruiting and a top-notch coaching staff.

The coach who had made Arizona State and Missouri powers in college football retained defensive coaches Paul Shoults, Joe Yonto and George Kelly. He also kept offensive coaches Greg Blache and Brian Boulac and added Ed Chlebek and Merv Johnson.

The recruits of 1975 were as highly regarded as those of

1973. Bob Golic, Steve Heimkreiter, Jerome Heavens, Rusty Lisch, David Huffman and Joe Restic all played their first games in 1975. Five players who had sat out the 1974 season also returned. The re-addition of Ross Browner, Willie Fry, Al Hunter, Danny Knott and Luther Bradley helped keep the Irish tough in Devine's first campaign.

But Devine wasn't without personnel problems that first season. He had to replace quarterback Tom Clements and needed help on defense for All-America candidate Steve Niehaus. Browner, Fry and Bradley were all professional material, but their year of inactivity diminished their effectiveness in the early part of the season.

In the quarterback derby were Frank Allocco (Clements' understudy in 1974), Rick Slager and Joe Montana. Slager, a fine option quarterback, came to the fore in the spring. His only drawback seemed to be his lack of height. But Slager had learned much from observing Clements. He usually stayed away from the big mistake and could move a team. Montana settled in as the back-up. He could throw as well as any quarterback on the team but was inexperienced and tended to throw costly interceptions. He also seemed to play his best every seventh day. Sunday through Friday he wasn't too impressive, but watch out on Saturday.

The squad of 1975 started the season on September 15 against Boston College in Foxboro's Schaefer Stadium. Five days later they faced Purdue in West Lafayette. A very tall order for any team.

Notre Dame came through with a 17—3 victory against the Eagles and a 17—0 win over the Boilermakers. In the latter contest, a ninety-nine-yard interception touchdown by Bradley pulled the game out of the fire.

Northwestern came to Notre Dame Stadium on September 27. Slager had started both games and did a very credible job. However, in the first half against the Wildcats, he was hit hard by defensive back Pete Shaw and was forced to the sidelines. Montana came off the bench to lead the Irish to a 31—7 triumph.

The first loss of the year came at home against Michigan State. The Spartans scored the only touchdown of the game with 3:50 left to give Denny Stolz's team a 10–3 upset win.

There was a significant rule change in 1975 that affected the next game. The limit of thirty grants-in-aid each year and a limit of ninety-five for the entire squad was taken one step further with a restriction on travel squads.

The Irish felt the force of the new rule when they traveled to Chapel Hill to meet North Carolina on October 11. The day was unbearably hot and humid. Late in the contest with the score tied, Notre Dame found itself eighty yards away from pay dirt and running out of fresh troops.

North Carolina was fired up from the beginning. The crowd roared on every Tarheel success, and it appeared that Notre Dame would be lucky to get out with a tie.

With the offense bogged down in the fourth quarter, Devine and his staff decided to insert Montana. His first pass was nearly intercepted deep in Irish territory. But a Carolina linebacker dropped the sure turnover, and Notre Dame still breathed hope; 1:03 showed on the clock as Montana threw a quick out pass to wide-receiver Ted Burgmeier, who juked and raced for eighty yards and the winning touchdown. Final score: Notre Dame 21, North Carolina 14.

So began the saga of the Comeback Kid, Joe Montana. The Irish escaped the Carolina hotbox and got ready to face Air Force the next week in Colorado Springs. The Falcons had never beaten Notre Dame, and the trip to the Rampart Range was supposed to keep that tradition intact.

But it was nearly a disaster. The rumors concerning Devine's status were renewed. It was reported that Don Shula of the Miami Dolphins would take over the team. Unsubstantial as they were, the rumors had to have some detrimental effect on the coaches and the team.

Ben Martin's Falcons did not have a good record but did possess some talented players. Linebacker Dave Lawson was one of the top placekickers in the nation, and Jim Miller later set an Air Force record for interceptions. Mike Worden at quarterback and Dave Reiner were the top offensive players, but the Irish were still heavily favored.

Air Force takes the opening kickoff and moves thirty-two yards before they are forced to punt. A thirty-nine-yard boot by Lange is blown dead at the Irish nine where the offense takes over. Slager gets the team two first downs on runs by Mark McLane and Terry Eurick, but Notre Dame punts from its own 45. Restic (who set a record for punting average in this game) hits a fifty-one yarder in the light air to Miller at the 14. Miller returns the ball twelve yards where Pete Johnson makes the stop.

Neither team can move the ball, and a Restic punt with 5:40 showing in the first quarter puts Air Force on its own eight. After going eight yards, Worden finds Bushnell for thirteen on a screen. The Falcon quarterback then completes a delay pass to Reiner for a thirty-nine-yard gain. Air Force takes the ball closer to the Irish goal but must settle for a forty-five-yard field goal by Lawson. It's an NCAA-record forty-third career field goal, and Lawson gives Air Force the lead in the early moments of the second quarter.

Notre Dame sets up shop on its own 30 and begins a drive. Heavens, Eurick and Jim Weiler pound the ball upfield but the Irish are checked on fourth-and-one at the Falcon six where McLane is dropped for a loss of two. Devine decides not to go for the almost sure field goal by Dave Reeve, and the Irish still trail by three with 9:17 showing in the half.

Air Force is stopped from any appreciable gain on their possession, and Lange kicks to Burgmeier at the Notre Dame 24. Burgmeier gets five on the return, but the Irish are hit with a clipping penalty. The mistakes have just begun to plague the visitors.

On the second play from scrimmage, a botched handoff results in a Falcon fumble recovery by Miller. It takes Worden one play to capitalize as he runs it over from the 16, and suddenly it's 10—0 after Lawson's kick.

The Irish get on the board after the kickoff when they drive the ball to the Air Force 13. The big plays in the march are a twelve-yard rush by McLane, a twenty-one-yard scamper by Heavens and a pass-interference call against the Falcons. The penalty occurs as Air Force intercepts, but the receiver is bumped during the play. Reeve's thirty-one-yard three pointer cuts the Falcon lead to seven with 3:12 on the clock.

Notre Dame gets the ball back with a new quarterback. Montana is in the game to see if he can get a quick score before the half ends. But Miller continues to pester Notre Dame as he picks off a Montana aerial. The pass was intended for Dan Kelleher on a fly pattern. Worden again finds Reiner on the delay pass, and the halfback takes the ball out to the Irish 46 for a twenty-five-yard gainer. Reiner gets twelve more on a draw before Niehaus makes the stop with three seconds left. Lawson comes out to kick his second field goal, and Air Force has a ten-point lead at half-time.

While Notre Dame has outrushed the Falcons, the edge in passing is the difference. The Irish have only seven yards through the air compared with ninety-nine for Air Force.

Worden has checked the rush of Browner, Fry, Jeff Weston and others with draws, delay passes and throws just in front of the linebackers. Although outmanned, the Falcons are frustrating Notre Dame by outguessing the Irish when it counts.

The Irish adhere to their offensive game plan (keeping the rush the main weapon) as Heavens scoots fifty-four yards on the fifth play of the third quarter. No one touches the freshman fullback as he goes into the end zone for the first Irish touchdown of the afternoon. Reeve converts, and it's 13–10, Air Force.

But again Miller makes another interception with less than twelve minutes left in the period. The Falcons have excellent field position with the ball at the Irish seventeen. On the first play, Worden fumbles but recovers for a gain of eight. The luck seems to desert the Irish as Air Force whittles the yardage down to the one, where Reiner scores around right end. Lawson adds the extra point and once again the Falcons have a ten-point lead, 20–10.

Following a Restic boomer of fifty-seven yards into the wind, Air Force starts another scoring drive from its own 20. Seven minutes and thirty-seven seconds remain in the third quarter.

Worden is flushed out of the pocket but scrambles for a fourteen-yard gain. He then links up with Froznea for thirty-nine yards on a deep post pattern, but Tom Lopienski saves the touchdown. At the Notre Dame 23, the defense holds, and Lawson hits his third field goal of the game making it 23—10 with 2:59 to play in the third quarter.

Irish mistakes are pushing the game out of reach. They continue to give the Falcons free points as Heavens fumbles on the first play after the kickoff. Linwood Mason makes the recovery and the corps of cadets senses that the greatest victory for the Academy is rapidly drawing near.

It takes Worden only three plays to get the touchdown. He hits Williams on the dead run for thirty-three yards and the third Falcon six-pointer. Air Force faced a third-and-sixteen situation, but Worden again made the big play when his team needed it most. The quarter expires with the home team in front, 30—10.

One minute and twenty seconds are gone in the last period when the Irish finally wake from their offensive slumber. Montana hits Kelleher for fourteen from his own 34, then finds tight-end Ken MacAfee for twenty-nine on a post pattern. The big receiver takes it to the Falcon eighteen. Three rushes by fullback Steve Orsini put the ball at the nine, where Montana keeps on an option over the left side and scores the touchdown. Reeve's kick is good, and it's 30—17, Air Force.

The quarter winds down to 6:56, when the Falcons apparently apply the coup de grace. Montana is intercepted when he tries to hit Kelleher at midfield. Miller sets sail for the Irish goal but fumbles at the Notre Dame 35, where tackle Pat Pohlen gets the ball back. It is a play that seems only a stopgap measure; but it turns out to be the key moment in a mistake-filled afternoon.

Just over six minutes remain when Montana finds wingback
McLane over the middle. Cutting behind the linebackers and
in front of the secondary, McLane runs across the field and
takes the short pass downfield for a sixty-six-yard gain. The
ball is at the Air Force seven. On the next play, MacAfee
breaks off the line and finds the ball waiting for him in the
end zone. Amazingly it's a six-point game with 2:59 left,
30—24.

**Ken MacAfee just after taking touchdown pass from Montana against
Air Force, 1975. Jim Weiler is at right.**

Reiner loses three on a run as Browner makes the hit. Two
incomplete passes force a Falcon punt. Lange gets off his
poorest kick of the day, twenty-eight yards. It's first-and-ten
for the Irish at the Air Force 45.

The first call is an option run to the right side. McLane wipes out the "contain man," which springs Al Hunter down the sideline. And, Hunter shows the Falcon defenders his heels. But he is robbed of a score as he's pulled down on the one-yard line.

Two plays later, Heavens tallies the third Irish touchdown of the quarter, and Reeve puts Notre Dame ahead, 31—30. Two scores in 2:06 have the Irish on top for the first time in the game.

Air Force moves the ball upfield as they have all after-noon. But on fourth-and-ten from their own 46, Lopienski breaks up a pass, and Notre Dame regains possession to kill the remaining moments on the clock.

The final 1:51 is gobbled up on six plays, and Notre Dame escapes with a one-point win. Twenty points in seven minutes and three seconds place the Irish in the win column for the fifth time in 1975.

With all the mistakes, the Irish decided to stay with their offensive game plan with a few varieties in the final quarter.

"We had run the ball well, and when Joe got confident, we knew we could score," recalled Merv Johnson.

"Some teams don't make that sort of comeback in thirty or forty years, and we do it in one quarter," said Devine.

Ed Bauer, a starting offensive guard, said confidence was renewed around Joe Montana. "It's just part of his total make-up. He just seemed to have that facility for rallying a team," Bauer said.

The 1975 team finished with an 8—3 record. It was a year of transition that was anything but easy. Dan Devine's first year turned out to be a tumultuous one, but two straight weeks of Montana magic prevented what could have been a disaster. The maiden voyage was not what many Irish fans wanted, but the stage was set for better days in the next five years.

8

PURDUE, 1977

"The Potboiler"

A blunt assessment of the Notre Dame team of 1977 was that they were loaded. Eleven defensive starters came back from the Gator Bowl team in addition to offensive stars like Ken MacAfee, Dave Huffman, Ernie Hughes, Dave Waymer and Kris Haines. A replacement had to be found for Al Hunter, who chose not to return to school for his final year of eligibility. Jerome Heavens was recovering from a knee injury, and Vagas Ferguson, while showing the promise that made him an all-American, had but limited experience.

Herein lies one of the strengths of the 1977 team. The defense showed talent everywhere, but the offense had to catch up. Helping out the players on offense were several unheralded stars who made vital contributions for the 1977 team. Terry Eurick, Steve Orsini, Tom Domin and Steve Schmitz were some of the players who did not possess the natural ability of some of the others, but got the job done.

In summer workout the Irish again faced the quarterback problem that had caused so much consternation in 1975. Rusty Lisch held the no. 1 spot with Gary Forsteyk and a guy named Montana in reserve.

The engineer of the great comeback wins over North Carolina and Air Force in 1975 had suffered a shoulder injury in practice before the 1976 campaign and sat out the entire season. He was rusty and a bit tentative before his junior year and had to bide his time.

Irish linebackers get ready for another afternoon under the watchful eye of assistant coach George Kelly.

The topnotch football magazines around the country recognized the Irish strength and projected them as the team to beat for the national title. The defensive exploits of Browner, Fry, Bradley, Golic, et al. were well-known. The defense, under coaches Yonto, Kelly and newcomer Jim Johnson, was expected to allow the offense to gain an identity while still winning ball games. It almost didn't happen.

The lid-lifter for the 1977 season had been moved to accommodate national television. Pittsburgh was under new head coach Jackie Sherrill who replaced Johnny Majors. A year earlier the Panthers had humiliated the Irish in Notre Dame Stadium on the way to a perfect season and national championship honors.

The game at Pitt Stadium saw Notre Dame in trouble early. The Panthers moved well with Matt Cavanaugh at quarterback. He took the home team to an early score, going to Gordon Jones for the six. But on the play, defensive end Fry hit the quarterback as soon as the ball was away. The perfectly legal hit was absorbed by Cavanaugh's wrist as he fell. The wrist was shattered, and the game suddenly got tight. It was a battle of frustrations with not much offense for either team. The Irish defense swarmed over the substitute quarterbacks, and finally Notre Dame escaped with a 19–10 win. But there was no escape the next week.

Mississippi got one of the biggest wins in its football history as they dispatched the Irish in Jackson by a score of 20–13. The Irish led late in the game, but the Rebs drove nearly the length of the field for the win. Notre Dame looked like anything but a national contender on that infernally hot day in Dixie.

The opponent for September 24 was Purdue. The yearly Big Ten rival always can be counted on to give the Irish fits. The Boilers always seem to throw a wrench into the Irish plans for a big season. Purdue in 1977 was not a typical Big 10 team of that time. They unveiled freshman quarterback Mark Herrmann to the football fans across the country by letting him do what he did best: throw, throw and throw some more.

But the phenomenon from Carmel, Indiana, was not the whole team. He had future NFL players like John Skibinski, Dave Young and Keena Turner to help him out. Purdue played a tightly controlled, yet highly variable defense that could put up nearly as many sets as the offense.

A bright and sunny Indian summer day greeted the overflow crowd of nearly 69,000 at Ross-Ade Stadium. Notre Dame could not afford a repeat performance on the road, or the national championship rings would be on another team's fingers over the winter.

Knowledgeable football fans know that the quickest way to let an underdog smell the upset is to turn the ball over via fumbles or interceptions. Very few games are played without some, but the adage, "Games aren't won, other teams lose them," is nearly always true in an upset.

Record-setting placekicker Dave Reeve begins the game by kicking off to Russell Pope. He returns it to the Purdue 18. Onto the field comes Herrmann, his number 9 jersey hanging awkwardly on a body that looks more like a marathon runner's than a college quarterback's.

Herrmann moves the Boilers to the Irish 49 before one of his passes is intercepted by free safety Joe Restic. But on Notre Dame's first play of the afternoon, Eurick gives the ball back to Purdue with Fred Arrington making the recovery. The game is not yet three minutes old and already the mistakes have begun.

With the ball on the Irish 32, Herrmann gets a break when pass interference is called on Notre Dame. The Boilers take it down to the eight, where on fourth down Scott Sovereen gives Purdue the lead with a twenty-five-yard field goal.

The Irish can't get the offense going and Kevin Muno, who has replaced the injured Restic, punts back to Purdue. Herrmann has good field position on his own 39 and uses only nine plays to complete his first touchdown drive against the Irish. The score comes on a pass to Reggie Arnold with 6:28 remaining in the first period. Sovereen's kick is good, and it's 10—0, Boilers.

The first period ends as Notre Dame begins to move the ball. Lisch re-enters the game after being replaced by Forsteyk. But Forsteyk leaves the game on a stretcher after a crunching blow by Arrington. Forsteyk suffers neck and shoulder injuries on the play, and the scene is a tense one as he is carried motionless from the field.

When action resumes it's third-and-ten from the Purdue 32 as Lisch runs for seventeen yards. The play gives the Irish their first scoring threat. A toss to MacAfee takes the ball to the eight yard line. Eurick loses two on a run but then grabs a Lisch aerial in the left flat for the first Irish score. Reeve converts, and Notre Dame trails, 10—7, with the second quarter just underway.

The tide appears to be shifting to the Irish as Herrmann is again intercepted, this time by Doug Becker. Becker picks the ball up at the Purdue 32 and the stocky linebacker nearly scores but is knocked down at the three yard line. A clip moves the line of scrimmage back to the 21, where Lisch strikes again. A pair of runs gains three, then the quarterback connects with Eurick again on a similar play for another score. Reeve splits the uprights and the Irish are up, 14—10.

A personal foul forces Reeve to kick off from the 25. Pope takes it to the 34, where Herrmann tries to get his team back in the lead. He hits tight-end Young for nine and for sixteen as the ball is at the Notre Dame 37. The next play finds Ray Smith isolated on linebacker Steve Heimkreiter. The linebacker falls, and Smith grabs the ball in full stride and gallops into the end zone for the touchdown. Ten minutes remain in the half as Sovereen kicks Purdue back to a three-point lead, 17—14.

The Irish start grinding out yardage after taking over on their own 9 yard line. Lisch hits MacAfee for ten, then Haines for thirty-two, but two misfires force a Muno punt, which carries to the Purdue 12 yard line.

The defense has the Boilers pinned but can't stop them from breaking out. Herrmann goes again to Young for fourteen. It's a first down at the Purdue 26. On third-and-nine, Herrmann bombs the Notre Dame secondary for a forty-eight-yard completion to Arnold. On the very next play, Herrmann lets fly again and finds Pope for the touchdown from forty-three yards out. The 24—14 count is what the Boilers take in at intermission.

Herrmann's aerial circus has been made possible by an offensive line that has kept Browner, Fry and company away from the quarterback. Given time, Herrmann can riddle any defense.

Notre Dame has moved the ball fairly well, but in comparison to Herrmann's 254 yards in passing, it will take much more to get the job done in this second half.

Offensive coordinator Johnson remembers the intermission:

"We knew we could move the ball and the defense would eventually get to Herrmann. We had to cut out the mistakes. Lisch had moved the team well, but I had Montana in mind, especially if things got worse."

The frustration of the Irish surfaces when unsportsmanlike conduct is called on them and the offense must start first-and-twenty-five from the Notre Dame 16. Ten yards are gained when Muno punts to the Purdue 35. The Boilers can't make up any ground and kick it back.

After a gain of twelve on a pass to MacAfee and two runs, Lisch's pitchout to Orsini is fumbled, and Marcus Jackson picks it up for Purdue on the Boiler 45.

Now the defense begins to assert itself. Ken Dike sacks Herrmann for a twelve-yard loss and the Irish get the ball via the punt, which carries to the Notre Dame 22.

But neither team makes a first down, and the clock winds down to near the half-way point of the third period. The Irish mistakes reach an unbelievable level when Lisch's pass for Waymer is filched with 2:21 remaining.

The ball is at midfield as Purdue looks to expand its lead, but defensive end Scott Zettek and Browner crash through the line to sack a now-hesitant Herrmann on his own 37. Dave Eagin punts the ball away; but from the Notre Dame 22, fullback Dave Mitchell can't hang on to the ball, and Lee Larkin makes the recovery. It's the fifth Notre Dame turnover.

The ball rests on the Irish 30 as Herrmann once again goes for the clincher. Golic tips a pass, but Mark Burrell makes the grab for an eighteen-yard pickup. The ball is at the ten where the defense digs in. Sovereen is called on to make the chip-shot field goal from twenty-seven yards out, but the Boilers are penalized for illegal procedure. The kicker misses wide left on the thirty-two-yarder. It's still 24–14 with seconds gone in the fourth quarter.

There are no fanfares from the Irish fans, but perhaps there should be. Joe Montana enters the game. He must make up

ten points and rekindle an offense's fire that has been doused
with turnovers and miscues.

As at Chapel Hill in 1975, Montana's first play is nearly a
disaster. Attempting to hit MacAfee, Larkins nearly intercepts
with nothing but wide open space between him and the
thirtieth Boilermaker point. But the linebacker can't make the
catch. Montana's warmup play is over, and now it's showtime.

He completes a pass to MacAfee for twenty-six, Haines for
twenty-five and gets a first down at the Purdue 29. An incompletion is followed by another strike to Haines for nineteen
and the Irish begin to roll. From the 10, the Irish gain four
yards. With 13:18 left in the game, Notre Dame is within
seven as Reeve pops through a twenty-four-yard field goal.

The Boilermakers get good field position on the kickoff, and
Herrmann is back to pass again. He hits Ray Smith for nine
and Skibinski for six. It's first-and-ten at the Purdue 48. Two
runs put the ball at the Notre Dame 40, where lightening
strikes again for a native Hoosier.

Herrmann tries to hit Arnold on a slant pattern, but the
pass is behind the receiver, and Luther Bradley intercepts on
the west sideline. Bradley, now a cornerback in his senior
year, sets sail for the goal. Herrmann, as he is falling, trips
Bradley at the Purdue 35, but the defense has once again made
a big play. In 1975, Bradley's interception had sparked the
Irish to their 17—0 win. It's happened again on the same field.

The thirty-five yards between the Irish and a tied game take
only two plays to be traversed. Montana, taking his cue from
a roused Irish defense, hits MacAfee for a twenty-two-yard
gain and then a thirteen-yard touchdown pass. The game is
tied at twenty-four, following Reeve's conversion.

Nearly 10:30 remains in the annual battle for the shillelagh,
but the tide is moving toward Notre Dame. The Bradley
interception followed by the quick touchdown has given the
Irish fans a reason to stay at Ross-Ade Stadium on this early
autumn afternoon.

Purdue tries to move its offense, and bruising fullback

Skibinski gives his best as he gains thirty-one yards on four straight runs. Herrmann throws incomplete, and Skibinski is stopped cold by Dike and Golic. The third-and-ten play is a key one. From Notre Dame's 49, Herrmann tries to link up with his tight end, but the pass is broken up by Burgmeier. Again the defense has held, and the offense will get the chance to maintain the momentum and move ahead.

But the Boiler defensive corps holds, and Muno kicks the ball to the Purdue 42. A holding call reverses the Boiler direction, but Herrmann is undaunted and hits Arnold for the first down at the Notre Dame 45. Purdue seems ready to go ahead again, but the critical penalty in the game is whistled against the Boilers on third-and-six from the Irish 41. An offensive pass interference flag costs the Boilers fifteen yards and loss of down. Notre Dame gets the ball back via an Eagin punt with 4:12 left in the game.

The previous two Purdue possessions take valuable time off the clock. There's now plenty of time for a long Irish drive that, if run properly, can get points and leave the clock wound down, forcing the Boilers to throw the ball deep to tie the game.

Montana brings his offense to its own 42-yard line and on the first play hits Haines for twenty-six yards to the Purdue 32. Mitchell, in the game despite his earlier costly turnover, hits the left side for two. Montana then finds MacAfee for four and gets the first down on a fifteen-yard completion to the big tight end. The line of scrimmage is the Purdue 11. Montana gives to Heavens for six and on second-and-four from the Notre Dame five, Mitchell jumps into the end zone for the game winner. As he tumbles over the goal line, Mitchell nearly drops the ball but hangs on in mid-air to score his first Notre Dame touchdown.

Reeve seals the Boiler's fate after the conversion as he booms his kickoff into the end zone. From the Purdue 20, Herrmann gets his team to the 46, but with time running out an incomplete pass on fourth-and-ten ends the Boiler offense for the day. The game ends with Montana losing two yards by falling on the ball.

It was another great job by Montana, and he gave the Irish of 1977 new hope in their push for a national title. The Notre Dame defense, highly touted all year long, withstood the aerial onslaught of Herrmann and shut down the Boilers in the second half.

Mark Herrmann had quite a day for a quarterback, much less a first-year quarterback. He appreciated the job his offensive line had done but realized that the second half was a different story. "I was hardly touched in the first half. I guess I took a few shots in the second half, but that's going to happen. In the second half it seemed as if their linebackers dropped off quicker and better. I couldn't get the ball in there."

John Skibinski played one of his best games ever at fullback for Purdue. He thought his squad had pulled off the upset. "When we had them down, I could see it in their eyes—we had them. When it changed, they got that spark, and it was like a whole new ball game for them."

Head coach Devine saw his team win another close game. The first three contests of 1977 all had gone down to the wire. The 1977 squad that was touted for national championship honors now was two and one, with two shaky victories and an upset loss. Still, Devine knew that his team was good and would get better. "We put in a gutsy performance today. We were missing a lot of people but refused to give up. It was a tremendous win for our staff. We hung in and hung in the entire game. Today was one of the best exhibitions of courage I have ever seen in a team."

Devine was asked whether all the publicity concerning his team and a national championship that was printed before the season had had an effect on the performance against Purdue. "We were a little looser today. I think our problems have centered around tightness and trying too hard to win. This sort of comeback victory will give us confidence now," the coach replied.

Besides Montana's heroics, the really big play was Bradley's interception of Herrmann's pass that nearly went all the way for a touchdown. Tom Dennin, who has broadcast Notre

Dame football games since 1969, remembers the play this way: "It was the breaker. After that the offense knew that they could get in and score. The whole game changed on that one play. It was just like 1975 when Luther Bradley ran back the interception for the long touchdown. They certainly didn't look like a national championship squad up until that point, but the confidence grew after that."

The Purdue game proved to be the turning point of the 1977 season. The Irish did not lose again. In fact, only two tough games in terms of score differential remained. They capped off the 1977 season by winning the national championship against Texas in the Cotton Bowl, 38—10. With Montana, Ferguson, Heavens and many others returning, 1978 looked once again to be a national championship or at least a national championship contending year.

Claim Number

213-835-4556 A11

5

USC, 1978

"Deja Vu"

Since 1900, only two Notre Dame teams have begun a season with a pair of losses. In 1963, on the way to a 2–7 mark, the initial defeats were administered by Wisconsin and Purdue. The loss to the Badgers came at Notre Dame Stadium. The 1978 team lost its first two games at home. To say the least, Irish fans were upset and bewildered.

But the 1978 season also proved that what sometimes starts sour, ends sweet. Or at least sweeter than originally anticipated.

The 3–0 loss to Missouri and 28–14 defeat at the hands of Michigan are interesting because neither probably should have occurred, but Notre Dame played so poorly that any major college team would have beaten the Irish.

Notre Dame had many opportunities to defeat the Tigers and led Michigan at halftime. But they surrendered the important third and fourth quarter battles to the Wolverines, and Bo Schembechler's crew departed Notre Dame Stadium with a victory.

Two plays from these games set a subtle tone for the remaining ten contests of the season. Against Missouri, Joe Montana hit Kris Haines on a flag pattern deep in Tiger territory. Haines had beaten defensive back Russ Calabrese on a

95

nifty route. Calabrese had made headlines the week before the game vehemently denouncing Notre Dame and just about everything concerned with the school. The remarks made him a marked man.

Noticing that he had beaten Calabrese, Haines tapped him on the helmet as he trotted back to the huddle. It was a grievous error. An official correctly penalized Haines for berating an opponent. And the mistake probably cost Notre Dame the game.

The key play in the Michigan game was Rick Leach's final touchdown pass of the game. The southpaw found Ralph Clayton on a post pattern and hit him in full stride for the score. But Clayton took a vicious hit from Joe Restic as the receiver made the grab. The game went to Michigan, but Restic left Clayton a little memory of Notre Dame Stadium.

Why these two plays? As defending national champions, the Irish had a great deal of pride. Calabrese's cheap publicity shot before the game brought out Mr. Haines' highly competitive nature. The explanation for Restic's defensive play was simple: Champs die hard.

The attitude of the Irish was if things didn't turn out well one week, get ready for the next. After the Michigan loss, Purdue was the first to fall, followed by Michigan State, Pitt, Air Force, Miami, Navy, Tennessee and Georgia Tech. In all of these wins, the Irish displayed a potent offense and a defense that was trying hard to overcome the loss of players like Browner, Fry, Becker, Burgmeier and Bradley.

Montana did not play well early in the season. But as the year went on, he got tougher. The turnaround was the Pitt game. Montana once again rallied the Irish to a win in which he completed big fourth quarter passes to Haines, tight end Dennis Grindinger and Vagas Ferguson. The latter also began to gain momentum toward a fine year of rushing. Teaming with Jerome Heavens, Ferguson helped form one of the best 1-2 punches in Irish backfield history.

The defense had ten players who later were either drafted or signed as free agents by the NFL. The team's only weakness was a secondary that could be moved against through the air. Ed Smith of Michigan State got twenty-five points teaming with Kirk Gibson, but strong safety Jim Browner made a key play with a fumble recovery (out of the arms of a receiver) for a touchdown. The longer the eleven men on defense stayed together, the better they got.

The Georgia Tech game in Atlanta is traditionally a difficult one for the Irish. The Yellowjackets have hurt the Irish twice at Grant Field (in 1976 and 1980) when Notre Dame was ready to push for national honors. But the '78 contest was all green and gold.

Montana had ten straight completions, Ferguson rushed for a then-record 255 yards and Notre Dame cruised to a 38–21 win. After the game, Notre Dame accepted a bid to return to Dallas for the 1979 Cotton Bowl. Many of the players waiting on the bus in Atlanta had hoped for a trip to Miami and the Orange Bowl, but when tendered the Cotton Bowl bid was readily accepted.

The team that lost to Missouri in September bore little resemblance to the one that left Atlanta with bowl bid in hand. Victories against USC in Los Angeles and against Houston in the Cotton Bowl would totally reverse the season.

The trek to USC was made by a team that was a much better squad but not in the greatest physical shape. Heavens and Ferguson were ailing as were linebacker Bobby Leopold and kicker Chuck Male. Since the expected close game might hinge on a kick, the deadly accurate Male, out with a leg injury, loomed as the costliest casualty.

The Trojans were having a fine year in 1978. Charles White, Paul McDonald, Kevin Williams, Pat Howell and Dan Garcia formed the core of an offense that lined up and pounded a defense while also setting them up for the passing game that struck short and long. The defense matched the offense in talent. Rich Dimler, Ronnie Lott, Riki Gray, Carter Hartwig and Myron Lapka came through with the big play that invariably got the offense in good field position for more points.

Unlike 1970, the weather was great in Los Angeles for the

November 25 contest. The match centered around Notre Dame's ability to slow the USC running game and the Trojans ability to keep Montana on the run and disrupt the passing game.

The Notre Dame—USC game of 1978 is remembered for many reasons: The unbelievable Trojan juggernaut in the first half, Irish injuries from the bruising contact along the line of scrimmage, Notre Dame's revitalized offense in the second half and a highly questionable call late in the game.

The fans in the Coliseum knew it would be a high-scoring game. Both offenses had highly sophisticated passing games and ground attacks that move the ball well.

Joe Unis, the diminutive kicker replacing Male, starts the game by kicking off to USC. The Trojans get one first down on a run by White, but their offense stalls when Golic sacks McDonald for a loss of eight. Marty King punts to the Irish who run but three plays before Restic punts the ball back.

McDonald begins on his own 28, mixing the run and pass well. The ball goes to the Irish 38 from USC territory on a pass to Williams good for forty yards. But Notre Dame's defense knocks away two more passing attempts and the Irish get the ball with 8:23 left in the first period.

The Notre Dame running game is stonewalled as Ferguson gets only two and Heavens one yard on the possession that begins on the Irish twelve. The ball control game moves toward USC as Restic is forced to kick again.

The Trojans begin their first touchdown drive from their own 45. White gets eleven on a pitch from McDonald, while the offense works to the Irish 30, where McDonald finds Williams open at the ten. The little speedster takes it into the end zone for a 6—0 USC lead. The extra point attempt fails with 4:32 left in the first period.

Both teams exchange punts after the kickoff. The Irish get their first points of the day when Montana, at his own 44, find Haines for a twenty-two-yard pickup to the USC 34. After two runs net four yards, Unis hits a forty-seven field goal. Both Irish and Trojans are stunned. Unis' kick was by far the longest of his career. The defense did not rush because they anticipated a fake. The score is USC 6, Notre Dame 3, as the first quarter ends.

The Trojans begin to use their brawn and ball carriers to move the ball. White zips inside left end for twelve yards out to the USC 41. Then McDonald switches gears and goes to the air. He finds Calvin Sweeney for twelve and with the ball at the Notre Dame 35, following a six-yard gain by White, McDonald gets his second touchdown pass.

Wide receiver Dan Garcia beats the secondary and hauls in the toss for the six points. The lefty quarterback then hits James Hunter for the two-point conversion. Just under thirteen minutes remain in the half as the Trojans lead, 14—3.

The quarter winds down to the midway point as USC starts another scoring drive. A nine-yard gain by White, a fifteen-yard penalty for roughing the passer and a Lynn Cain run for twelve yards set up Frank Jordan's thirty-nine-yard field goal, making the score 17—3, USC.

The Notre Dame offense is rolling in reverse. Following the kick-off, Montana loses nine, back to his own nine-yard line. With 2:48 left, Restic punts again. USC holds a fourteen-point lead at intermission, with the statistics frighteningly in their favor.

The Irish are lucky to be down by only fourteen. They have a total of minus three yards rushing and but three first downs. Their total offensive output is but fifty-nine yards. USC has 247 total yards. White has gained seventy-eight yards on the ground himself.

McDonald is hot in the passing area with ten for eighteen totaling 163 yards. Montana is unbelievably ineffective so far, with but three completions in fifteen tries.

Notre Dame cranks up the offense and makes its fourth first down of the game after Ferguson and Heavens split the necessary yardage. With third-and-eight from his own 32, Montana finds Haines. The receiver is interfered with at the USC 41 for another Irish first down.

Montana gains more confidence as he links up with Heavens

out of the backfield for a sixteen-yard gain and another first down at the Trojan 28. A screen pass to Ferguson gains eleven to the USC twelve where the march sputters. Unis hits another field goal, this one good for twenty-six yards, and it's 17—6, USC. Notre Dame got some points on the board during their initial possession of the third quarter, but USC will steal any momentum that may have been gained by the visitors.

McDonald has his offense in high gear. He finds White in the right flat for fourteen and Sweeney for twenty-two and a first down at the Irish twenty. White rolls for thirteen over the left side, and the Notre Dame defense, minus Golic and Mike Calhoun who are injured, is reeling. Seven minutes and thirty-eight seconds remain in the third period as White leaps over from the one yard line for the touchdown. Jordan converts, and USC has a 24—6 lead.

The Trojans are now a cocky bunch on the sidelines as television cameras record their revenge from 1977's thirty-point drubbing at the hands of Notre Dame. But Montana and Company still have twenty-two minutes to do something about the eighteen point lead.

From the Notre Dame 22, the lanky quarterback marches his team for an apparent score as he takes the Irish down to the USC one-yard line. The big plays in the drive are a twelve-yard completion to Haines, a nine-yard toss to Dean Masztak, a ten-yard rush by Pete Pallas and an eleven-yard reception by Haines. But on second-and-goal from the one, Montana fumbles as he tries to sneak the ball into the end zone, and Notre Dame comes up dry. This development causes some Irish fans to head for the exits. The jinx that has haunted Notre Dame ever since the 1966 51—0 win over USC apparently will continue.

The quarter ends with USC on the march for another score. This one would put the game out of reach. McDonald, having the best day of his career, hits Vic Rakhshani for twenty yards to the Notre Dame 33. White continues his impressive day on the ground as he picks up twenty-one more yards against an Irish defense that can do nothing to stop the

Trojans. USC gets the ball to the Irish four-yard line, where Notre Dame gets a break. Jordan inexplicably muffs a field goal, the equivalent of an extra point. The score remains 24–6, Trojans.

The missed field goal is all the Notre Dame offense needs as an impetus. Montana hits Masztak for twenty-three yards down the middle, and from the 43-yard line Montana goes for all the marbles. Haines beats his defender and streaks down the left side of the field behind the secondary. He takes the pass on the USC 15 and canters into the end zone for the first Irish touchdown. The Irish fail to make the two-point conversion, and the score is 24–12, USC. Just over twelve minutes remain in the game.

The Trojans can't score but do the next best thing. They consume almost six minutes of the remaining time; 6:56 shows on the clock as Montana leads the offense from the Notre Dame two-yard line on first-and-ten.

It's the beginning of a masterful drive for a score. Montana hits Haines for seven yards on a quick out pattern. Heavens gets four, and it's first-and-ten at the Irish 13. Montana has regained the confidence that enabled him to be one of the best quarterbacks in the country during the '78 season. He connects with Haines for twenty yards and then a nineteen yard pickup. It's first-and-ten at the Southern Cal 48 as Masztak takes a pass down the middle for seventeen yards and Haines is the recipient of an eighteen-yard gain. Montana has found his touch, and the Trojans are reeling on defense. Holohan gains eighteen on a pass reception as does Haines, and it's first-and-ten at the Trojan thirteen. After losing five on a busted play, Montana breaks from the pocket and scampers for fifteen yards. It's first-and-goal from the Trojan three yard line.

Freshman fullback Pete Buchanan crashes over from the one yard line for the touchdown. Unis kicks the extra point, and Notre Dame is within five at 24–19. Three minutes and one second remain in the game.

The Irish defense, knocked around all afternoon, rises to the occasion and gets the ball back by limiting Southern Cal to five yards in three plays. King punts out of bounds at the Irish 43.

One minute and forty-three seconds are left in the game as the teams, crowd and millions viewing the game on television wonder if Montana can do it again.

He runs for five yards around right end and then hits Ferguson for a four-yard gain. The quarterback gets the first down by picking up three himself. From the USC 47, he finds Ferguson out of the backfield down the right sideline for twenty-four yards and a first down at the Trojan 21. Holohan is interfered with at the USC 12. Montana finds Mazstak for ten yards to the two-yard line, and it's another first down. Forty-eight seconds remain as Montana fires a bullet to Holohan in the end zone on a quick slant pattern. Holohan is mobbed as the Irish lead, 25—24. Haines can't grab the two-point conversion pass, and Notre Dame must hold the one-point lead with forty-six seconds left.

USC begins it's last gasp drive on its own 30. McDonald hits Rakhshani for ten and a first down at the 40. The quarterback tries to throw again, but Jeff Weston and Joe Gramke pour in on McDonald, who loses control of the ball. It bounces to the turf where Notre Dame recovers. Instant jubilation by the Irish! But referee Paul Kamanski rules it an incomplete pass. McDonald appeared to have lost the ball as he ducked to avoid Weston, but the referee's call stands.

Given new life, McDonald hits Sweeney for thirty-five on a crossing pattern in front of the Irish secondary. White gains four, and with two seconds left, Jordan comes onto the field to attempt the game-winning field goal. The thirty-seven-yard attempt is good. Trojan fans embrace their team as USC has gone fifty yards in less than a minute. The Irish comeback is but a memory as the third loss of the season is recorded against Notre Dame.

USC coach John Robinson knew he had been in a historical game as he talked with reporters.

"It's the greatest game I've ever seen, but maybe every USC–Notre Dame game is. It was as hard a hitting game in the first half as I've ever seen. A lot of people got hurt," he he said. "We had our own tackles going in and out of the game. It was just a very hard-hitting game."

The Trojan coach, who had taken over for the legendary John McKay, also praised his opponent. "Notre Dame came back like most good teams do. They came back as fine as I've ever seen. But we did it too. When you have two great teams battling out there, you can expect things like that to happen."

Why was Notre Dame able to gain such massive amounts of aerial yardage in the second half when they were stymied in the first half? Offensive coordinator Merv Johnson explained. "USC ran a multitude of coverage against us. They have very good talent. They tried to take away all of our patterns and just limit us to a few. Montana got his confidence with Haines. Kris adjusted his routes a couple of times

A strategy session between quarterback Montana and offensive co-ordinator Merv Johnson.

and we made connection. We knew we would get in a tight game if Montana would regain his confidence."

But the nagging question in both locker rooms was the fumble or incompletion that occurred late in the game. Irish coach Dan Devine, who had seen his team come back from almost sure defeat to grab a lead with less than one minute remaining, discussed the controversial play: "I didn't see the pass at the end. It was a crucial decision, so I can't comment on it. But if it was a bad decision, then that was the ball game. Again, I haven't seen it, so I can't comment on it. But if the referee made a mistake, he should never work another game. In our locker room there are a bunch of youngsters bitterly disappointed—he's caused my kids a lot of pain."

The referee who made the call, Paul Kamanski, is a veteran collegiate official. He discussed the crucial call with Dave Condon of the *Chicago Tribune*:

"I reacted to what I saw. I can still see it. The pass hit a Notre Dame rusher, making it incomplete. I'd make the same call again."

Kamanski did make the call quickly. Many people believe that was the only saving grace on the judgment call. Many also believe he made the call too soon. The game ended with a victory for USC. But the statistics compiled by the Notre Dame comeback corps in the second half were excellent. Montana ended the game with twenty completions out of forty-one attempts for 358 yards and two touchdowns. His counterpart, McDonald, also had a fine day, with seventeen completions out of 29 attempts for 281 yards. The southpaw quarterback, now with the Cleveland Browns, talked about the final drive that produced victory for his team:

"We had two time outs left for that final drive, and that goes to show you how much forty-six seconds is. We've prepared for this [the last minute offense] all year and never used it till now."

Kris Haines had his best day as a collegiate receiver. He made nine catches good for 179 yards and one touchdown. "In the second half, they played me man-to-man, and I got to feel more comfortable as the game went on. They allowed me to run my patterns, and Joe got me the ball," said a dejected Haines after the game.

But Notre Dame still had one more game left to play and they would begin 1979 as they had in 1978: in Dallas playing in the Cotton Bowl. This time not for national honors, but for pride.

10

HOUSTON, 1979

"The Icing on the Cake"

The crushing disappointment that beset the Notre Dame team of 1978 had to be rectified and reversed quickly. The Cotton Bowl bid that had been accepted before the disappointing loss to USC pitted the Irish against the University of Houston on New Year's Day, 1979.

A multi-faceted enigma faced Dan Devine's crew after the loss to the Trojans. They had one more chance to complete their season-long reversal and go out winners. The players would tell themselves that only on the scoreboard did they lose in Los Angeles. The seniors wanted desperately to leave Notre Dame with a string of three straight Bowl wins. But few members of the team wanted another trip to Dallas.

The Cotton Bowl is one of the truly great post-season games. The people of Dallas and the Cotton Bowl Committee go all out to show the teams and their fans a great time. The Irish had won the national title in Texas over the state's favorite college squad. But there are no beaches in Dallas, no night life like New Orleans and no national championship on the line for the 1979 Cotton Bowl.

Yet there was one character trait the Irish of 1978 had in abundance that made them a respected representative of Notre Dame. The pride that enabled them to rebound after two losses, to come back against Pittsburgh and USC and get ready for Houston served them well against the Cougars.

Tri-captains Heavens, Montana and Golic had done a fine job in leading a team that had survived one of the most dismal starts in Irish history. They each represented a distinct facet of the team and gave each member of the squad a captain with whom to identify.

Montana led by example. His talent on the field was more than enough to inspire a player. But Montana was not haughty or aloof despite the enormous pressure and attention that was with him throughout the season. Golic led the defense from its heart, middle linebacker. He showed a dramatic amount of perserverance as he battled to get ready for Houston following the injury he sustained in the USC game. Heavens had come back from a serious knee problem in 1976 to break the rushing record held by George Gipp. But in 1978, Heavens yielded the ball-carrying center-stage spotlight to Vagas Ferguson without any loss of effort, production or dedication. Few players have served their teams better as captains.

Notre Dame's opponent in the game could probably identify with Rodney Dangerfield. The Houston Cougars were the new team on the block in the Southwest Conference. In each hostile stadium shouts of "Cougar High School" and "Bandits, bandits, bandits" greeted Bill Yeoman's team. Still Houston won against more established schools in the conference by using the original veer offense and a defense that played a reckless, no-holds-barred, frontierlike game. The Cougars of 1978 had plenty of talent. Danny Davis was the archetypal option quarterback. Lean and lanky, he could throw well enough to keep opposing secondaries on the lookout for something more than veer right or veer left. Randy Love, Emmet King, Ken Hatfield, Willis Adams, Hosea Taylor and David Hodge joined Davis to lead the Cougars against the Irish.

Notre Dame got ready for the game in a different manner from the way they prepared for the 1978 Cotton Bowl. Coach

Devine gave his team more time off, and practices were not as intense.

The weather for January first in Dallas is usually ideal for football. It's more like fall than the dead of winter and plenty of sunshine usually bathes the fans in the stadium. The first day of 1979 was an exception to the rules governing weather, football and logic.

An ice storm blew into "Big D" on the night of December 31 and brought the city to a standstill on the morning of the first. Ice hung like frozen strands of laundry on power lines. 50,000 homes in the city were without power. But the game was played before whoever had the courage to sit through the numbing cold that cut through the Cotton Bowl like a scythe.

The artificial turf was glazed with ice as the teams hit the field. The temperature hovered around the 20° mark, but the wind was the worst. It raged from the northwest at 15–20 miles per hour with gusts hitting nearly 45 miles per hour. The wind-chill factor, a familiar indicator to the Irish fans, was even a little severe for the northerners. The kickoff took place with a chill factor of −6°.

The Irish win the toss and change their decision twice before deciding to receive. Randy Harrison takes Hatfield's kick and gallops fifty-six yards to the Houston 34, putting the Irish offense in good shape on its first possession. The offense eventually faces fourth-and-one, when Heavens is stopped for no gain by Hodge, and the Cougars take over.

Three first downs are made on runs, but Notre Dame gets the ball back as Love fumbles at the Irish 38, where defensive end Jay Case recovers. From his own 35, Montana faces a third-and-nine as he finds Heavens out of the backfield for a twenty-seven-yard pass completion. In Cougar territory, Montana goes airborne again and finds tight-end Dean Masztak for a gain of twenty-six to the Houston six-yard line. Three plays later, Joe gets the score on a one-yard run. But the Irish fumble the center snap on the conversion, so it's 6–0, Notre Dame.

Steve Cichy's kick is taken by Terry Elston, who fumbles on

the 25 yard line. Freshman linebacker Bob Crable recovers, and the offense goes back on the field. Six plays are used to get the second Irish touchdown. Montana's connection to Ferguson for nine yards, a run by Vagas for eight more and a seven-yard advance by Heavens are the big plays. Pete Buchanan gets the score as he dives into the end zone from a yard out. The Irish fail to make the two point conversion, and it's a twelve-point spread for the Irish. Four minutes and forty seconds show in the first quarter.

The Cougars get two first downs but must punt when Case and Jeff Weston drop Davis for a two-yard loss. Jay Wyatt's punt is ruled touched by Dave Waymer, who is deep to receive. Waymer appears to have eluded the kick, but possession goes back to Houston on the Irish twelve. Two plays later, Davis hits Adams for the first Cougar score. Hatfield's extra point is good, and the score is 12—7, Notre Dame, as the first quarter ends.

The Irish punt the ball away on their first offensive set in the second quarter, but Randy Love fumbles on the second Cougar play and John Hankerd makes the recovery. The Houston veer, at best a high-risk offense, is not working in the icy and wet playing conditions.

But Notre Dame can't move either, and punts are exchanged. The Irish have the ball on their own twelve yard line and get it out to the 22, where Montana fumbles the center snap, and Houston takes over deep in Irish territory. It is still difficult for the Cougars to move against the Irish defense, but the representatives of the southwest finally go ahead as Love scores from a yard out. Six minutes and twenty-three seconds are left in the first half as Hatfield converts. It's 14—12, Houston.

The problems of the second quarter continue for Notre Dame as Montana is intercepted by Hatfield as he throws long. The defensive back takes it from midfield to the Irish 25. Houston scores again in six plays as Hatfield hits on a twenty-one-yard field goal, making it 17—14, Cougars, with a little more than two minutes left in the second period.

There is no return on the kickoff, and the Irish begin on their own 20. Heavens gains seventeen on first down and takes a pass from Montana at the Houston 46 for another first-and-ten. But at midfield, Montana is intercepted by Steve Bradham, who takes it to the Irish 49.

The Cougars note the clock and with three seconds left, Hatfield kicks another field goal to give Houston a 20—12 lead at halftime.

The Irish have been lethargic in the second quarter, not able to overcome the elements and bad stretch of ball handling that cost them the lead. Former Irish All-American and Heisman Trophy winner Paul Hornung, providing color commentary for the CBS television viewing audience, is quick to note this. "Notre Dame looks lackadaisical, and Dan Devine will have a job on his hands to key up the players this cold day for this second half," he says. The Golden Boy's observations are correct as Notre Dame's poise against the wind and Houston's fired-up defense was not the best in the world. The Irish are only eight points down but have to get it rolling.

But there is more than just being behind at the half that troubles Notre Dame. In the exertion of the first two quarters, Montana's body temperature has dropped suddenly and dramatically. He is chilled and shivering as Irish trainers and physicians cover him with blankets and coats to help get his temperature back to normal in the locker room. If Montana does not warm up, he will not play any more this afternoon.

"They told us Joe was not coming back in the second half, and we thought it was over, but we've learned over the last four years that it's never over," said center Dave Huffman, a native of Dallas. His words would be prophetic for the final two periods of football on a terrible afternoon in Texas.

The Irish retake the field and on their second possession are pinned deep in their own territory. Dick Boushka punts for thirty-two yards, and Houston begins at the Notre Dame 38.

King fumbles and recovers for a loss of ten, but seven plays later Davis keeps on the vecr into the end zone for the touchdown. It's 27–12 after Hatfield's kick, and 7:31 shows in the third period.

Tim Koegel takes over for Montana, but there seems to be nothing he can do to change the lack of Irish luck. The misfortune continues as Boushka has his kick blocked on his own 19-yard line. The ice-covered field and howling wind make any airborne ball an adventure and a mystery.

It takes Davis only three plays to negotiate another score. The rangy quarterback keeps on a five-yard scamper, and Hatfield's boot extends the Cougar lead to 34–12, with 4:44 left in the third stanza. Houston has answered the initial twelve Notre Dame points with thirty-four of their own, and they're rolling. It is highly unlikely that a team, no matter how courageous, can make up twenty-two points on a day when the elements are so harsh.

As the Irish prepare to receive the kickoff, Montana goes back on the field. Applause would be in order, but chilled hands prevent any ovation. Still his teammates know he would not have come back if he were not ready to go. And when Montana is ready to play, something good usually happens for Notre Dame before the time on the clock expires.

Montana's wide receiver, Kris Haines, remembered what he thought when the familiar no. 3 came back onto the field. "Here he comes again. He's done it so many times before, but this time it's got to be a miracle."

Montana's debut, as are most of his appearances when playing the comeback role, is less than auspicious. One incomplete pass bounces off an official's head. Another interception is thrown, and Houston begins the fourth quarter with the ball on their own eleven yard line. The only thing the Cougars lose as the quarter ends is the wind, but that will prove crucial. Both teams are forced to punt on their first few offensive possessions of the fourth quarter. It fits with the Houston game plan as the clock, one thing that is not frozen, moves down to 7:37 remaining in the game as Wyatt prepares to kick against the wind from his own 33.

The Irish return team pours in on the Cougar punter, and

Tony Belden blocks the kick. The ball flutters downfield where fellow freshman Cichy grabs it. He struggles and suddenly breaks out of the pack and streaks for the end zone. It's a touchdown on the blocked punt and return. Two close friends, Belden and Cichy, have made one of the many big plays in this game.

"We just knew as we lined up we were going to block the kick. I wasn't touched; it was like a dream," said Cichy. "I couldn't believe I was so wide open. I had a player holding onto both ankles, but I broke both of their tackles."

Montana finds Ferguson for the two-point conversion, and Dan Devine's team is within fourteen points. Now the defense must get the ball back.

The Irish, while always playing quite well against the wishbone offense, have had their trouble with the veer. Defensive coordinator Joe Yonto explains the adjustments the Irish made in the second half: "We had to shut off the quarterback. The added flanker gave us problems to the outside. The veer hits quicker, so we hit quicker. It was just a matter of us controlling the line of scrimmage when we had to."

The defense allows the Cougars nine yards as Wyatt manages to get off the kick this time back to Notre Dame. There is no return as the Irish offense begins on its own 39. The chicken soup Montana gulped at halftime must have found a place in his right arm as he heats up the passing game.

He hits Masztak for seventeen, Heavens makes a fantastic grab for thirty more and after pass interference is called on Houston, it's Notre Dame's ball with first-and-goal from the three. Montana scrambles around left end and slams into the end zone for the touchdown. The two-point conversion is good as Haines breaks his pattern and comes across the end zone to make the grab in the middle of three Cougar defenders. It's 34—28, Houston, with 4:22 left in the game.

The Cougars need only a few first downs to "ice" the win. Love rips off a sixteen-yard gain on first down, but Houston is detected holding. On third-and-eight, Davis finds the Irish secondary in man-to-man coverage and tries to throw for the first down. He has Adams isolated and open against Waymer. The ball is in the receiver's hands as Waymer flies through the air to flip it to the ground for the most critical play by the defense, at least so far. Wyatt punts to midfield with 2:25 left.

Montana hits Haines on a sideline pattern but is sacked on the second down for a loss of six. The quarterback locates flanker Pete Holohan on another sideline pattern for a fourteen-yard gain and a first down at the Cougar 36.

On the next play, Montana is flushed from the pocket and takes off toward the Houston goal. But as he hits the twenty yard line a pursuing defender knocks the ball out of his hands. The fumble is picked up by the Cougars with but 1:50 showing.

"When I saw Hodge coming, I made a move to elude him. I had the ball in my hand because I had forgotten to tuck it away, and somebody tackled me from behind," said Montana. A dejected, disappointed and downright mad quarterback heads to the sidelines. Offensive coordinator Merv Johnson, who has engineered the Irish comeback so far, assures Joe that the game is not over and that the defense will get the ball back. They will have at least one more try. Montana looks forlornly at Haines and says the game is all over. Haines is not so sure. "I told him it wasn't finished yet. We still had some time."

The Irish defense has to stop the clock by using time-outs with 1:38 and :46 left. On fourth-and-six the Irish, attempting to block the Houston punt in a last-gasp effort, are offside. It's now fourth-and-one from the Houston 29.

Yeoman decides to apply the crusher. He goes for the first down as Davis gives to King on the dive play. Those who see the result will never forget it. Defensive tackle Mike Calhoun destroys the interference, leaving King face-to-face with end Joe Gramke. The freshman stands up the ball carrier and gives away nothing. Steve Heimkreiter is also there to help. King has hit a wall of Irish pride, guts and topnotch defensive play. There is no gain. The ball goes over to Notre Dame with twenty-eight seconds left.

"We expected their best back to get the football, and we

Joe Gramke makes The Hit, stopping Houston on fourth and one to give the ball back to the Irish.

guessed right. Gramke was right there and made a perfect tackle. He kept his feet moving, and the back did not," said Yonto.

The Cougars look for the pass as Montana runs for eleven and a first down. Notre Dame has no time-outs left. As the ball is marked ready for play, Montana gets Huffman's snap and fires to Haines just inside the right sideline for ten more yards. As he goes out of bounds, Haines blasts a Cougar defender with a vicious forearm. The fire is far from doused.

Six seconds remain as Montana misfires going for Haines. The play uses only four seconds. Time for one more play.

Montana consults with coaches Devine and Johnson on the sidelines. A quick out pattern is called for. It's a three-step drop pass. It must work; it will be the last play of the game.

"Joe asked me if I could beat the man again, and I said yes," remembers Haines. "He smiled and said, 'Let's do it.' " Montana eludes the rush and fires a bullet to Haines who has come back for the football. As he cradles the pigskin to his chest and falls over the end-zone sideline, Haines' foot is still in bounds. Coach Johnson remembers that Ferguson was also a primary receiver. "The outside linebacker did not go out, there was no depth to his drop on the pattern. Vagas would have been open if Kris hadn't come back so well for the ball."

Irish fans are ecstatic. All that is now needed is for Joe Unis to kick the extra point and Notre Dame is a last-second victor. The ball is snapped to Greg Knafelc, who gets it on the tee and Unis' kick flutters through the goalposts. But the Irish are called for a penalty. Unis must do it again, this time from five yards farther away.

"I just tried to put all the screaming, yelling and jumping around out of my mind. You just think of the basics, keep your head down and kick it. I didn't have time to think about being nervous. Every kicker fantasizes about winning games like this," recalls Unis. The snap on the second attempt is not as good as the first. Knafelc makes a fine play as he somehow manages to get the ball into place for the kick. The rush is awesome. The ball is nearly blocked, but some-how Unis powers it through the uprights again. No flags. Victory for Notre Dame, 35—34 in an unbelievable finish to an unbelievable afternoon.

The cold was forgotten as the Notre Dame locker room erupted. The seniors had their three straight bowl wins. It was a scene that no one will ever forget. Haines remembered the biggest catch that he will ever make in his life: "It looked low and outside, but that's where it was supposed to be. It's my job to catch it. This is the greatest feeling in the world. I'll

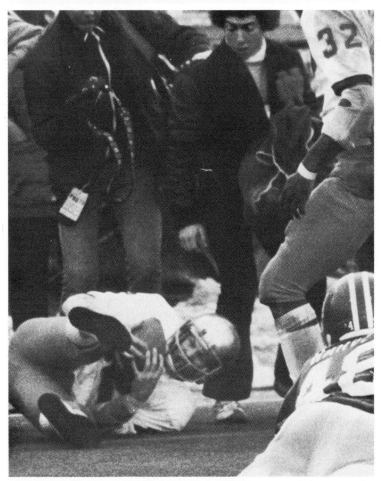

The Cotton Bowl comeback is nearly complete as Haines hangs on for the tying points. His right foot remains in bounds. Vagas Ferguson looks on with astounded sideline fans.

remember it for the rest of my life. This team never quits, and when we blocked the punt, we knew we could come back."

Coach Devine commented on his quarterback who once again had done the seemingly impossible. "What makes him the leader he is? You saw it today. He proved it to me in the third game of his sophomore year. On our depth charts he was listed last, behind even the walk-ons. That's why Montana is as good as he is. He never quits."

The members of the media in the Houston locker room had to ask Coach Yeoman about the controversial call in which he went for the first down instead of punting. "We were kicking the ball ten or twelve yards into the wind, and Chuck

Coach Dan Devine is congratulated by defensive secondary coach Jim Johnson after the 35-34 comeback against Houston in the 1979 Cotton Bowl . . . South Bend Police Sergeant Cullen Walton looks on.

Brown had a bad wrist and couldn't snap the ball. I was completely responsible for that call.

"The kids played hard and played well. It was a pretty good season. We've been having good victories for the past ten years, and this could have been another one. But it was just an extremely hard loss," said a dejected Yeoman, whose team came back to win the 1980 Cotton Bowl.

The Houston players were in a state of shock. They had seen a 34–12 lead evaporate. "We didn't let up, we just sat on the lead against a team that comes back," remembered linebacker Hodge, who was voted the game's Most Valuable Player on defense.

Defensive back Tommy Ebner was wondering what happened and if it was really of this world. "Maybe we did relax there for a little while. But I'm not going to say that Irish luck stuff didn't run through our minds. I couldn't believe it."

It will be many years before college football will see a rally the likes of that which occurred in Dallas on January 1, 1979. Great plays abounded amid the mistakes and the bad weather. But the greatest play may have been by Joe Montana, when he didn't spill a drop of the chicken soup at halftime. And he isn't even Jewish.

11

SOUTH CAROLINA, 1979

"Better Late Than..."

Football historians don't know what to make of the 1979 season. Was it a success or failure? Most Irish fans believe a 7–4 season is a disaster. But the '79 campaign proved not to be terrible or tragic.

The ugly specter of injuries cast a shadow over the Irish even before they faced Michigan in the season opener. Pete Buchanan, the talented sophomore from nearby Plymouth, Indiana, suffered a serious break in his lower leg in the final pre-season scrimmage. Buchanan had been expected to relieve some of the pressure on running-back Vagas Ferguson, who was destined to become the all-time leading ground gainer in Irish history.

Injuries hit at quarterback, in the defensive line and the defensive secondary. Even the kicking game was affected by injury. Injuries today have a greater effect on team performance than they formerly did. One reason may be the imposition of grant-in-aid limitations. The NCAA has decreed that only thirty grants may be offered in one season, and the total number may not exceed ninety-five. This is the main reason college football has become more balanced and team depth has been reduced.

The Irish were still an exciting, offensively explosive team in 1979. The first win of the year, against Michigan in Ann Arbor, raised Irish hopes that the youthful squad could make a run at national honors. Notre Dame upset the Wolverines with Chuck Male kicking four field goals. The twelve points were just enough to edge Bo Schembechler's team, 12—10. A last-second block of a Michigan field goal by Bob Crable gave the Irish the win. Vagas Ferguson had begun his All-American season by running for 118 yards through the Wolverine defense. Defensive linemen Don Kidd, Scott Zettek and Kevin Griffith all played well in the narrow win, as did cornerback Dave Waymer and strong-safety Steve Cichy.

But quarterback Rusty Lisch injured his ankle late in the game and was forced to miss the Purdue game the following week. Reserves Mike Courey, Tim Koegel and Greg Knafelc took the Irish to a 20—7 lead at West Lafayette, but again an injury changed the outcome. Waymer hurt his knee in the second half, and the Boilers' Mark Herrmann seized the opportunity to pick apart the Irish secondary in the fourth quarter for a 28—22 win.

After victories over Michigan State, Georgia Tech and Air Force, Notre Dame suffered its second loss of the year to a more talented and experienced Southern California team. The Rose Bowl-bound Trojans handed the Irish a 42—23 loss at Notre Dame Stadium. The Irish offense, paced by Lisch and Ferguson, did just about everything possible to win. But the defense could not stop Charles White on the ground nor the passing of Paul McDonald, as John Robinson's team broke loose in the second half to win the game.

South Carolina came calling to South Bend on October 27 for a game that saw the Irish as favorites. The Gamecock defense was not expected to stop Ferguson, and although talented, the South Carolina offense was inconsistent and usually plagued by turnovers.

The game served as a showcase for several stars and future All-Americans. The action was one of the hardest hitting, tightest games played in college football during the 1979 season. Although it was not sharply played for four quarters, none could doubt the effort put forth by both units.

After opening punts by both teams, the Irish offense goes to work. Freshman wide-receiver Tony Hunter teams with Lisch for the first big play. One of the best all-around athletes ever to play for Notre Dame, the 6'5", 215 pound Cincinnati native is a legitimate game breaker from any position on the field.

Six minutes and twenty-one seconds remains in the first period; Lisch hits Hunter for a thirty-nine-yard completion down the west sideline. Hunter gets behind the defender and expertly comes back for the ball, which is slightly under-thrown. Falling as he makes the catch, Hunter cradles the ball for the completion, and the Irish are in business.

Ferguson fails to gain, and Lisch throws to fullback Ty Barber for a twelve-yard gain to the Carolina 29. Two incompletions make it third-and-ten as Lisch hits tight-end Dean Masztak for a six-yard gain to the 23. Chuck Male trots out and drills a forty-yard field goal out of Koegel's hold, and Notre Dame leads, 3—0.

The Notre Dame offense has moved via the accurate right arm of Lisch. A fifth-year senior enrolled in the architecture program at Notre Dame, Lisch had been a capable replacement for Rick Slager during the Alabama game in 1976 as he preserved the 21—18 win with two big bootleg runs in the second half. A year later, Lisch was replaced by Joe Montana as the starter in the Purdue game. He continued to serve as Montana's understudy in 1978 and waited for the 1979 season when he would be the main signal caller.

South Carolina takes Male's kickoff and moves to their own 49 as the first quarter ends. Sophomore linebacker Bob Crable is in on nearly every play for the Irish. Crable, smaller and quicker than the graduated All-American Bob Golic, had inherited the middle-linebacker spot due to his tremendous enthusiasm and ferocity. In 1979 Crable was still a year away from being the complete linebacker that just about everybody had expected when he came to Notre Dame from Cincinnati's Moeller High School. Crable ranged from sideline to sideline on this dark October day, being in on an incredible twenty-six tackles. His linebacking partner, Mike Whittington, now of the New York Giants, would have twenty-one hits.

Notre Dame's defense forces another punt as does the Gamecock defense. Dick Boushka of the Irish and South Carolina's Eddie Leopard take center stage as the kicking game holds sway.

The Irish defense pounds away at 1980 Heisman Trophy winner George Rogers and his running mate Spencer Clark. Their battering-ram style cannot break out against Crable, Whittington and strong-safety Cichy. The first half ends with Notre Dame still leading by the margin of the Male field goal.

After intermission the Irish offense that had sparkled against Southern Cal continues to stop itself with fumbles, penalties and dropped passes. The Gamecocks seem ready to take control of the contest. Rogers has plugged away for sixty-four yards on fourteen carries, and the running game is slowly beginning to wear on the Irish defense. The sluggish South Carolina running game has turned into a constantly moving force; still, the Irish defense has not allowed a point.

In the third quarter South Carolina strikes quickly with little warning. Quarterback Garry Harper is an option signal caller who does not throw often nor very well. On the Gamecocks' first possession of the second half, Harper switches gears and stings Notre Dame.

Harper hits receiver Zion McKinney on a slant pattern that is designed to gain seven or eight yards, but the fleet McKinney turns it into a sixty-two-yard score as he splits the Notre Dame secondary and legs it in for the tally. The extra point is good, and the Irish trail, 7—3.

The lightning-like touchdown seems to anesthetize Notre Dame. After a Boushka punt, Spencer Clark bursts through a gaping hole in the Irish line and bolts forty-nine yards for another Gamecock score. Suddenly it is 14—3 with Notre

Dame on the short end. The Irish defense, which had hit so well in the first half, now looks infantile against a team that has not shown much but is quickly beginning to believe it can upset Notre Dame. Carolina adds a thirty-three-yard field goal off the toe of Leopard, and it is 17–3 with less than two minutes left in the third period.

The game continues to move away from the Irish as the Notre Dame offense tries to recover. A Lisch-to-Barber completion gains nineteen, and a Holohan reception for twenty-two gives the crowd something to cheer about. Phil Carter, who took over for Ferguson in 1980, runs for seven yards, and the ball is on the Carolina 26. Seventeen seconds remain in the third quarter.

If there is a forgotten man for Notre Dame this day, it is Vagas Ferguson. He has gained only thirty-one yards in the first half, and the quick Gamecock defense makes Ferguson a marked man from the opening kickoff. Yet great players often wait for just the right time to make their presence felt; such is Ferguson on this day.

Lisch pitches the ball to no. 32, and Ferguson puts it in high gear as he tightropes the west sideline, heading for the south end zone. A super block from guard Tim Huffman springs Vagas loose, and twenty-six yards later Notre Dame has its first touchdown of the afternoon. Male's extra point is true, and the Irish trail, 17–10.

Notre Dame seems to have awakened but knows it will be a long struggle if they are to triumph. As Ferguson later explained, "We were thinking of nothing but winning going into the fourth quarter. We certainly didn't want to bear the humiliation of defeat."

The final period turns out to be a defensive chess game. Crable, Cichy, Whittington and end John Hankerd keep Carolina from breaking any more big plays, but time is slipping away. Rogers must fight for each yard he gains, but the Gamecocks are holding onto the football. Harper relies on his big running backs to gain yardage and time.

The Irish must eat up a lot of yardage to get into position

All-time leading Irish rusher, Vagas Ferguson. Now of the New England Patriots.

to sustain a tying land drive if necessary. One big play would allow Ferguson and Carter to punch the ball into the end zone or set up a Male field goal. From his flanker position, Holohan takes a Lisch handoff and lofts a long pass to speed merchant Ty Dickerson. The ball is in Gamecock territory at the seventeen. The drive stalls, and Male attempts a thirty-four-yard field goal. Usually deadly accurate throughout the

...'s winning drive against South Carolina in 1979 is culminated as Dean Masztak hauls in the winning score from Rusty Lisch ...ohan pulled in the clinching two point conversion mo-

past two seasons, Male misses, and Carolina gets the ball back. The Notre Dame defense holds and forces a punt, but so do the visitors, and time is on their side.

Less than two minutes remain as Jim Carlen's team moves the ball into Irish territory. Two first downs are all the Irish give up, and Carolina faces a fourth-and-two decision on the Notre Dame 41. The Gamecock offense wants to go for the clinching first down, but Carlen and his staff decide to allow the defense to make Notre Dame move the ball the entire length of the field. Carolina coaches and players spend too much time debating the merits of each option. For the first time in the game, the clock catches up with Carolina. The delay-of-game penalty decides the issue, and the punt carries into the end zone for a touchback. With 1:36 remaining, Notre Dame gets the ball for possibly the final time.

The Irish defense watches intensely on the sideline. They have played well for the most part but had known early in the game that they were not too keen, that they had not forced the big break.

"After the loss to USC, we were lackadaisical. We didn't have a good week of practice. We hit well, but that was about it," said Steve Cichy.

"We had held them, but time was going fast. I really didn't think we could do it. But the offense had played well against USC, and I was hoping," explained the strong safety.

It has been said that the measure of a good quarterback is the ability to defy the physical laws of time and distance. Johnny Unitas had this uncanny ability. His precision sideline passes to Ray Berry seemed to occur when the clock had ceased to function. Each college and pro team, and most good high-school teams, practice what is known as the two-minute drill. It is used when a team must go a long way in a very short period of time. There are no long bombs, only strategic running and short-pass plays, and several plays are called at one time in the huddle. Sometimes the offense will not use the huddle at all; the quarterback will bark the plays at the line of scrimmage. The Irish offense is twenty-four seconds shy of a real two-minute situation, but Lisch does not need that much time.

He connects with Pete Holohan for twelve yards, again for fifteen and to Dickerson for eighteen. On the catch by Dickerson, the Indianapolis native steps out of bounds stopping the clock. No official time-out is called, and Lisch next hits Ferguson out of the backfield for eighteen yards and another first down. Vagas cuts back to the middle of the field and is finally brought down by a swarm of Carolina tacklers. Lisch calls time and heads for the Irish bench.

Jim Gruden, the offensive backfield coach, is in contact with quarterback coach Ron Toman. Toman is overlooking the field from his press-box-spotter location. Along with Dan Devine, Lisch huddles with Gruden, who relays Toman's suggestions. It is down to the final minute. A sideline pattern pass is called. If they complete the pass, the receiver can quickly get out of bounds. If no open man is found, Lisch must throw the ball away to stop the clock.

Notre Dame is driving the ball toward the northern end of the stadium. The students there rain down cheers as the Irish prepare for the final push.

Lisch throws for Holohan, but the pass is over the flanker's head. The next play is a microcosm of the entire afternoon. Lisch fades, looks downfield and lets fly. The ball is batted by a Gamecock defensive lineman directly back to Lisch. Ever on the alert for the unexpected, Lisch makes the catch and tries to run but is quickly tackled. Thus, Lisch is credited with a pass completion and reception on the same play.

Notre Dame takes its last time-out with forty-eight seconds left. Lisch is instructed to call a pass play that involves all five receivers in the pattern. Before the huddle breaks, Lisch has special instructions for his tight end, Dean Masztak.

"Rusty called the play in the huddle, but then gave me different instructions," said Masztak. "He told me to hook up in the end zone and the ball would be there."

Third-and-seven from the Gamecock fourteen turns out to be very lucky for the Irish faithful. Masztak hooks around his

Rusty Lisch gets ready to fire against South Carolina, 19 man in the end zone after breaking free from the line who has lined up directly in front of the tight end on line of scrimmage.

Lisch drills a bullet that Masztak jumps slightly fo latches onto for the touchdown that sends Notre Da Stadium into a frenzy.

Rusty Lisch gets ready to fire against South Carolina, 1979.

man in the end zone after breaking free from the linebacker, who has lined up directly in front of the tight end on the line of scrimmage.

Lisch drills a bullet that Masztak jumps slightly for and latches onto for the touchdown that sends Notre Dame Stadium into a frenzy.

Notre Dame's winning drive against South Carolina in 1979 is culminated as Dean Masztak hauls in the winning score from Rusty Lisch ...Pete Holohan pulled in the clinching two point conversion moments later.

"It all happened so fast, I really didn't have a chance to think about it," remembered Masztak.

Dan Devine knew that the pattern called would make his tight end the perfect and primary receiver. "[We] sent both of our backs out in the pattern to control their linebackers. That helped get Dean open," Devine said.

Still the Irish trail by a point. Few if any of the 59,075 in attendance even remotely think the Irish will go for the equalizer. It is incomprehensible. Notre Dame will win by one or lose by one. Devine was quite emphatic about his strategy.

"I've never gone for a tie in my life, and I never will. I didn't come to Notre Dame to tie," he said.

"You can't play the tie. You just can't do it. I knew when I heard the play for the two-point conversion that we had it," recalled Steve Cichy.

With the crowd roaring at the decision for all or nothing, Lisch brings the team to the line with the game riding on the execution of the play. He surveys the defense and decides to change the call.

But it is a change for the best. After a pump fake, the ball flies out of Lisch's grasp and travels like a beam of dark brown light to a pre-arranged spot to the west side of the north end zone.

Pete Holohan does not see the ball leave Lisch's hand. He still has his back to the quarterback as Rusty fires. When his final step hits the turf, Holohan makes a quick left turn and looks for the ball that must arrive precisely at the same moment as Holohan's turn. The pattern had been practiced nearly ad infinitum before and after each Irish workout.

It is truly an example of the art that is an integral part of sport. The pass, Holohan and two points arrive on schedule. The flanker leaves his man as the cut to the outside is made, and all Pete must do is make sure he has the ball. He does and exits the end zone with the game-winning catch, jumping and running back down the sideline toward the Irish bench. Holohan never breaks stride as he is engulfed by joyful teammates as Notre Dame Stadium is once again up for

grabs. Fifty-four seconds have elapsed since Lisch took the
snap on the Carolina twenty.

The Gamecocks still have a chance but as Whittington
breaks up a desperation pass from Harper, the game goes into
the victory column for the Irish, 18–17.

Members of the Irish defense celebrate as the last South Carolina
drive is stopped. Left to right: Bob Crable (43), Tom Gibbons (facing
camera), Mike Whittington (54), and David Waymer (34).

Vagas Ferguson finished the day with ninety-four rushing
yards. It was well below his seasonal average, but Ferguson
had expected the attention that he received all afternoon.

"They could have beaten us, but we wouldn't let them.
They were just what we expected," said Ferguson, who had
the bruises and welts of seven tough games crisscrossing his
shoulders, legs and chest as he talked with reporters after the
game.

Lisch, as usual, did not say much after the game. A quiet,

deeply religious man, Lisch saw the game and the final drive as merely an outgrowth of a situation that had been anticipated since the beginning of practice in mid-August.

"It was just a matter of going out and doing what we do in practice, doing what we had to do. That's the two-minute drill."

Gamecock head coach Jim Carlen, who rebuilt the football fortunes of Texas Tech and South Carolina, had seen the elation of a late win and now faced the alternative.

"It wasn't the stadium or the mystique that beat us; it was the players. We just couldn't slow them down in the last few minutes," responded Carlen as his players silently showered and dressed around a tomb-like locker room.

The Irish returned to earth the next week as they scraped by Navy, 14–0. Two more losses prevented a bowl game and forced fans to wait until 1980 for more football success at Notre Dame. The comeback in the South Carolina game, along with the Michigan cliffhanger, were the high watermarks of 1979.

Vagas Ferguson finished the season with 1,437 yards and a career total of 3,472. He still holds the top two seasonal rushing marks (1978 and 1979). His seventeen rushing touchdowns is also a career mark that stands. Ferguson was drafted in the first round by the New England Patriots and set a rushing record for a Patriot rookie. He always seemed to have a flair for the dramatic, even if he was unassuming off the field. Ferguson battled inclement weather to make the dinner to attend a banquet for retiring Coach Dan Devine. When Fr. Edmund P. Joyce called on Vagas to speak, he had just entered the Athletic and Convocation Center arena. But he strode to the dais as if he had been there throughout the evening.

The St. Louis Cardinals drafted Rusty Lisch in 1980. Against long odds, Lisch made the team as a back-up quarterback to Jim Hart. For Lisch the two-minute drill is part of his job. But on October 27, 1979, Lisch only needed fifty-four seconds to make the two-minute drill a work of art.

12

MICHIGAN, 1980

"Oh Harry!"

In November of 1887 a group of eager and enthusiastic Notre Dame students contacted some of their fellow collegians at the University of Michigan about bringing the new game of football to South Bend. It was fitting that the Irish (as they would eventually be called) asked the Wolverines for lessons. Michigan was the undisputed "Champion of the West" (a term that has lived on as part of the Michigan fight song, "The Victors".)

The Notre Dame *Scholastic* recorded the action: "Because of the recent thaw, the field was damp and muddy, but the players of both sides plunged into the play with no regard for their cleanliness or comfort. . . . the scrimmages at first were between sides chosen irrespective of college. After several minutes of this practice, play was halted, players returned to their respective sides and the real game was begun.

"Since the game had to be finished by noon, it was limited to one period of 30 minutes' duration. This resulted in a score of 8–0 in favor of Michigan on two touchdowns. The game was interesting and has started an enthusiastic football boom. It is hoped that coming years will witness a series of these contests."

The writer of those words had no idea of the understate-

132

ment that his story would become. After the first game in 1887, both Michigan and Notre Dame achieved outstanding football success over the decades.

The big names over the years of high football fortune for Michigan were Yost, Crisler, Oosterbaan, Harmon, Ford (Gerald R., All-American center and thirty-eighth President of the United States), Elliott and Glenn E. "Bo" Schembechler. While the Michigan success may not have been of the national scope as was Notre Dame's, Wolverine teams were among the best year in and year out for many seasons.

But the Irish and Michigan played only thirteen times between the instructional game in 1887 and 1980. There are two main reasons why the two powerhouses have met so infrequently. Michigan is a member of the Big 10 Conference while Notre Dame is an independent. Under Rockne and Leahy, the Irish shunned regional play, preferring to play from coast to coast to spread the school's reputation and allow as many people in as many areas as possible to watch Notre Dame in action.

The Maize and Blue held a 10–3 advantage when the two teams were scheduled to meet in the second game of the 1980 season for both teams. The series had been renewed in 1978 at Notre Dame Stadium when Michigan came away with 28–14 win after trailing at halftime. The following year, Michigan fans were shocked as their team was beaten 12–10 at the huge Michigan Stadium.

The coaches of the teams were at the top of the profession in 1980. Bo Schembechler had built winner after winner at Ann Arbor. His teams were renowned for hard-hitting defense and an offense that relentlessly drove the ball down the field with ball control the watchword in the Wolverine game plan.

If Schembechler had a fault, critics said that he was too conservative and failed to win the "big game." Dan Devine, who had announced August 15, 1980, that the coming season would be his last at Notre Dame, stood second (behind Bear Bryant) in coaching wins among the active coaches in 1980. Yet Devine had endured almost constant criticism from Irish fans

who did not see him as a proper successor to the likes of
Rockne, Leahy and Parseghian.

Both teams were coming off mediocre 1979 seasons. A so-so
7—4 year for Notre Dame and an 8—4 ledger for Michigan,
with a loss to North Carolina in the Gator Bowl, left fans per-
plexed as the first football season of the new decade was about
to begin.

There were question marks for both squads entering the
season. Notre Dame had lost All-America running back Vagas
Ferguson, tackle Tim Foley and pro draftees Bobby Leopold,
Dave Waymer and Rob Martinovich. The Wolverines would
not have the likes of Ron Simpkins, Doug Marsh, Mike Jolly
and Curtis Greer; 1980 would seemingly be a make-or-break
year for both teams.

Both teams chalked up victories in their first game on
September 20. Notre Dame look unbelievably impressive in
dispatching Purdue, 31—10. Irish skeptics pointed out that
All-America quarterback Mark Herrmann did not play, but
the Irish so totally dominated the game that Herrmann's
presence may have tightened the action but would not have
changed the outcome. Michigan had squeaked past Northwestern, 17—10, in a game that was contested in a downpour
that rendered both teams' offense helpless.

The Wolverines had their most explosive team in many
years. Anthony Carter, a sophomore from Florida, looked
more like a gymnast than a football player but his mercury
moves made him one of the most dangerous players in the
country. Butch Woolfolk was one of the top runners in the
Big 10 and linebacker Andy Cannavino stopped just about
everything that came his way.

Notre Dame gained a huge amount of confidence in its big
win over Purdue. Phil Carter took over the mantle of tailback
from Ferguson with authority while Mike Courey displayed
calm confidence in leading the Irish to their first win of the
season. On the defense, players who had been thrown into the
fray during the 1980 campaign, were now veterans and could
hold their own with the best offenses in the nation. Bob
Crable was headed for All-America honors, while end Scott

Phil Carter finds a hole.

Zettek was making his final year one to remember. The game promised to be a classic.

Still the game did not have the big buildup that many had expected. The Irish had not convinced everyone that they were a top team in 1980, and the narrow seven-point win over a weak Northwestern team gave cause for concern among Wolverine fans. There was little or no hint that the September 20 game would be a game that is still talked about.

Both teams used similar offenses going into the contest. The tailback was the main weapon in both attacks, with options for the big play with Carter for Michigan and Tony Hunter for Notre Dame. The defenses, expected to be the strong point of both teams, would have to try and hold on as the offense of both squads would take center stage.

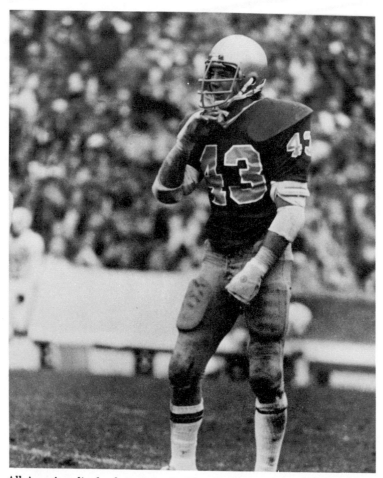

All-America linebacker Bob Crable. Twice voted captain by his teammates.

In the modern game of football there is an offensive unit, a defensive unit and special teams. The latter are the most overlooked aspect of college football and perhaps the most important over the course of an eleven- or twelve-game season. The ability to run back punts and kickoffs and to limit your opponents' ability to do the same can win games for a team. A field goal at the proper time could make a lead safe or force an opponent to try and keep the ball away from an offense, that while not necessarily potent, was good enough to make the three pointers add up.

The day is warm—unseasonably warm for South Bend in late September. But a light wind from the south tends to gust, making it a pleasant afternoon for football.

Notre Dame takes the opening kick but must punt the ball. Freshman Blair Kiel, one of the most heralded first-year players in the nation, does not get off a good boot and Michigan takes over on its own 45. Rich Hewlett, a sophomore quarterback, is at the throttle for Michigan. He can only move the team three yards, and Schembechler calls for his punt team. Don Bracken, also a freshman, booms the ball into the end zone, and the Irish must start from their own 20.

Mike Courey is the main man for the Irish as they begin their second possession. He scrambles for three as his receivers are covered, rolls to his left and loses one and scrambles again for seven yards before being downed at his own 29. Michigan takes the punt and begins to move. Beginning the drive on their own 33, Schembechler's men take it down to the Notre Dame 29. Larry Ricks, taking over for Woolfolk, who has an injured back, gains thirteen yards on two carries while Stan Edwards accounts for eleven. Ali Haji-Sheikh is called on for a forty-seven-yard field goal. He makes good contact, but the attempt fails; already the kicking game has come into play.

Notre Dame takes over on its own 30. The new start of the Irish running attack is Phil Carter. The tightly wound scat-back runs for nine and four, and Courey has his first first down of the game. Courey alternates Carter and short passes to move the Irish downfield. There is nothing pretty about the Notre Dame drive, but a young offensive line is beginning to fire out well against the 5—2 defense of Michigan. The first quarter ends with no score.

The Irish offense works the ball to the Wolverine 21 as Courey passes on the slant pattern to Hunter for eleven. Now the partisan crowd senses the first dent on the scoreboard. After minor penalties to both teams, Carter gains four to the

Michigan six. The Notre Dame offensive line of Mike Shiner, Rob Gagnon, John Scully, Bob Burger and Phil Pozderac has moved out the Maize and Blue defenders, enabling Carter to run and Courey to mix in high-percentage passes to his talented receivers: Hunter, Dean Masztak and Pete Holohan.

The ball is at the Michigan six with second-and-goal as the indefatigable Carter is given the ball and plunges over the goal line for the first score of the game. Thirteen minutes and five seconds remain in the first half.

The Irish line up for the extra point. Tim Koegel, who has been a back-up quarterback for three years, is the holder. The kicker is Harry Oliver. He has been an understudy to Chuck Male and Joe Unis. He nearly lost his grant-in-aid because he had not shown enough improvement in his kicking. But he has risen through the ranks of the Irish kickers. Bill Siewe's snap is true, and Oliver swings his left leg through the ball. Notre Dame leads, 7–0.

Mike Johnston, one of the kickers whom Oliver beat out for placement duty, kicks off, and Anthony Carter fields it in the end zone for a touchback. The Michigan offense can only gain seven yards, and Bracken punts to Dave Duerson, who returns the kick six yards to the Irish 49.

With the lead, Courey looks to Hunter again; his pass is incomplete, and the Irish are penalized seven yards for illegal use of hands. After a one-yard gain by Phil Carter, Courey goes to Hunter for a sixteen-yard gain. The quarterback, used primarily in running situations, is using the pass to move the Irish downfield. Tailback Carter gains eight, and fullback John Sweeney picks up six. With the ball inside the Wolverine 30, Courey goes to the ground to move it closer to the goal. After moving the ball to the 20, Courey throws to Masztak for a gain of eight. Notre Dame inches the ball down to the Michigan ten and a time-out is called by Courey. The defense has had to concentrate on Notre Dame's powerful running game and a change of pace is in order. Quarterback coach Ron Toman, backfield coach Jim Gruden and Devine huddle with Courey before deciding on a quick pass to flanker Holohan.

The same player who had caught the winning pass on the two-point conversion against South Carolina in 1979 does it again. He catches Courey's pass in the eastern corner of the north end zone. Holohan's break is perfect, as is Courey's pass, and the Irish have another score. Oliver's kick is good, and it is 14–0 with five minutes left in the half.

Michigan responds as would any championship team. Carter returns the kickoff thirty-one yards to the 32 and their offense begins to roll. The big play is a twenty-eight-yard gain by Ricks up the middle. Safety Rod Bone makes the stop, but the Wolverines are in business at the Irish 26. John Wangler has taken over for Hewlett at quarterback. He is the best passer among Michigan quarterbacks, and his pass to Anthony Carter sends the Wolverines down to the eight-yard line of the Irish. Wangler rolls to his right and tosses to running back Ricks for an eight-yard touchdown pass. The 14–7 margin is the same as Notre Dame had in 1978 before Michigan came back for a 28–14 win behind Rick Leach.

One minute and fifty seconds remain as the Irish get the ball back. Courey goes for Hunter but the pass is incomplete. Another pass is intercepted by Marion Body in front of the Irish bench, and the Wolverines have the ball back with 1:30 remaining before intermission.

The ball is at the Irish 21 as Wangler goes to work. He moves the line of scrimmage six yards but is faced with a fourth-and-four. Michigan is well within the range of Haji-Sheikh, but Bo Schembechler is anything but conservative with the play calling. Hewlett comes in to hold for the field-goal try but passes to fullback Edwards who makes an acrobatic catch to move the ball to the twelve. Wangler re-enters the lineup and throws to tight end Norm Betts for the second Wolverine touchdown of the afternoon. The point after is good, and the game is tied.

After the kickoff, Courey is again intercepted by Body, but the clock runs out before the Wolverines can score, and the first half ends at 14–14.

Both teams have moved the ball quite well in the first two quarters. The two interceptions by Body have clouded a fine performance by Mike Courey and the Irish offense. Notre Dame controlled the ball for eighteen minutes and twenty-nine seconds in the first half, but is deadlocked with the opportunistic Maize and Blue at the conclusion of the first thirty minutes.

The first half had seen almost a complete reversal of momentum within a matter of moments. After Holohan's touchdown reception, Notre Dame seemed to lose its direction. Schembechler's insertion of Wangler had as much to do with the Wolverines coming back from the two touchdown deficit as any other factor. The Michigan offense could now move through the air as well as on the ground. The Wolverine defense had proven opportunistic with the two interceptions by Body. The first portion of the game had belonged to Notre Dame, but Michigan had stolen the thunder.

Mike Johnston kicks off for Notre Dame to begin the second half. Anthony Carter takes the ball on the one-yard line and waits for his blocking to form. The return is set up for the west sideline. As the Irish defenders seem to have Carter hemmed in and prepare for the tackle, the little speedster makes nearly a 90° cut and begins to head across the field. His speed suddenly sets him free with yards of open field ahead. The only Notre Dame player with a chance to catch Carter is Rod Bone. The sophomore cannot match the speed of the ball carrier and tries to cut down the distance by stretching the angle. Bone's tactic works, and Carter is hogtied after a sixty-seven-yard gain to the Irish 32 yard line.

Wangler goes to work and moves the ball against the shell-shocked Irish. Running backs Edwards and Ricks move the ball behind the massive Michigan line and advance it to the Irish seventeen. Wangler switches gears and passes to Edwards for an eleven-yard gain to the Irish six. A play later the Wolverines score as Edwards plunges over from the two. The conversion is good, and Michigan leads for the first time in the game, 21–14.

The Irish are penalized for clipping on the kickoff and have horrible field position to begin their possession. On

third-and-four, Courey loses four, and the Irish are backed
up on their 17. But freshman Kiel gets off a tremendous punt
of sixty-nine yards that carries all the way to the Wolverine
18. Anthony Carter returns it to the 26. The punt has
rescued Notre Dame for the moment.

Michigan is forced to punt after moving the ball to the
45. The biggest play in the series is a thirteen-yard completion
to Anthony Carter. But it is the last time the lithe wide
receiver will touch the ball in the game. The Notre Dame
secondary has been extremely physical with Carter throughout
the afternoon, and after making the reception, he is hit hard
by free safety Tom Gibbons. The pounding tackles have
bruised Carter's ribs, and he is little more than a decoy for
the remainder of the game.

The Notre Dame offense finds no room to move, and
crucial penalties halt any direction upfield. With the ball on
the 12 yard line, Kiel comes in at quarterback. He quick-kicks
the ball for another great boot. It's a fifty-nine yarder, and
the Irish are out of a hole again.

Three minutes and forty-three seconds remain as Wangler
leads his offense back on the field. He hits Ricks for nine,
Edwards picks up five, and it's a first down at the Michigan
40. Defensive end Jeff Lueken, in the game for a more effec-
tive pass rush, does his job as he sacks Wangler for a loss of
seven. The ball is on the 34 with a third-and-sixteen situation
as Wangler fades to throw. He looks for Carter who cuts
across the field looking for the ball.

The Irish pass rush closes in on Wangler, who fails to read
his receiver's break. Lueken and Pat Kramer nearly have
Wangler sacked, but the ball is thrown toward Carter. Strong
safety Tom DeSiato, playing in place of the injured Steve
Cichy, and cornerback John Krimm are covering on the play.
Krimm had been forced to play much of the 1979 season with
a broken hand that had limited his effectiveness. At the last
possible moment, Krimm cuts in front of Carter and grabs
the ball. One of the fastest players on the team, Krimm is at
full speed after a few steps. He is nearly to the east sideline

when he cuts back toward the middle of the field. He does not break stride as he picks up blockers, and as he passes Wangler, he is free. The Columbus, Ohio, native high steps it into the end zone, and Notre Dame is within a point.

As described by John Fineran of the *South Bend Tribune* the following day, Krimm had been told of his good fortune by teammate Bone.

"He told me that he [Bone] dreamed I would intercept a pass and return it for a touchdown," said Krimm.

In describing his big play, Krimm gave his front line credit. "Carter started to curl but read the coverage and broke to the outside," related Krimm. "The quarterback got a strong rush and didn't read the break."

The extra point would have deadlocked the game at twenty-one, but it didn't happen. Harry Oliver forgot to point his toe and follow through. The Irish still trail by one with one-minute-and-three-seconds remaining in the third quarter.

Michigan is forced to begin the series at the ten yard line after a personal foul on the kickoff. The Irish defense, sparked by Krimm's play, allows only three yards, and Bracken is forced to punt. Dave Duerson takes it near midfield and moves it into Michigan territory as the third quarter ends.

The Wolverine defense is just as tough and limits Notre Dame to but three yards as the last period begins. The Michigan offense cannot move nor can the Irish, and the Wolverines get the ball back at their own 46.

Butch Woolfolk, the best of the Maize-and-Blue backs, hits the line for a total of sixteen yards on four carries as Wangler, now back in the game after being pulled following his ill-timed pass, moves the club. But Crable tackles Wool-folk as the back tries to sweep around the right end. Woolfolk fumbles, and Duerson recovers.

The Irish must come up with a big play as half of the fourth quarter is gone. Courey hands the ball on a suspected end-around play to Tony Hunter. The talented split end, who had played a little quarterback in high school, pulls up and fires downfield for Holohan. The flanker has only single coverage, and he hauls down the bomb for a gain of thirty-one. The offense now has new life. Courey hits tight end Masztak for ten, Phil Carter gains nine, six, one and another six-yard pickup to give the Irish first-and-goal at the Michigan eight. Senior Jim Stone moves it down to the four when Carter comes back into the lineup and leaps into the end zone behind a crunching block by Pete Buchanan to put the Irish ahead. The offensive brain trust of coaches Devine, Gruden and Toman decides to try for the two-point conversion. Courey's pass is incomplete, and the Irish lead, 26–21.

The drive that began with the Hunter pass and ended with Carter's dive consumed four-and-a-half minutes. The Wolverines get the ball back on their own 22 with less than three minutes remaining. No one expects that a run-oriented team without its top receiver could travel the seventy-eight yards to win the game. But Wangler utilizes his running backs and clicks with Woolfolk for a twelve-yard gain. Woolfolk gets the ball on a draw play and breaks through the line for a twenty-yard gain. As he is hit by Zettek, Woolfolk fumbles, but Michigan's John Powers recovers the ball.

Defensive tackle Don Kidd, who has battled star-center George Lilja to a draw all afternoon, is forced to leave the lineup as Michigan is faced with but 1:06 left on the clock and forty yards to go for the score. High percentage passes are in order, but once again Woolfolk busts loose on the draw and is quickly into the secondary. Kidd had clogged the middle for the entire day, but was on the bench as the play went right past the area he had so expertly patrolled. Two nifty moves past Irish defenders propel Woolfolk past the defense. Only a shoestring tackle by Gibbons saves the touchdown. It's a thirty-seven-yard gain and the ball is on the Notre Dame four.

The Irish defense refuses to give up the easy touchdown and gives up but three yards in two cracks by the Michigan offense. Wangler calls time-out with forty-nine seconds left and confers with Schembechler and quarterback coach Gary Moeller.

Michigan is using two tight ends to aid in blocking for the

run, but on a play fake, Wangler fades to throw. Notre
Dame's secondary has everyone covered, and the rush comes
at Wangler. He throws a wobbly, end-over-end pass that
deflects off Woolfolk's hands and tumbles toward the back of
the end zone. Craig Dunaway, the second tight end in the
game, is trailing the play. He lunges for the ball and grabs it
for the score. The Irish fans fall suddenly quiet for it appears
Michigan has pulled off the last minute win. Wangler tries
for Dunaway on the two-point conversion, but the pass is
incomplete. Forty-one seconds remain in the game as Haji-
Sheikh's kick goes through the end zone.

Dan Devine makes a critical decision at this time. He
inserts Kiel into the lineup for Courey. Kiel can throw long
better than the senior, but it is the first snap he will take
where he does not have to punt the ball. Bill Siewe replaces
John Scully to make the long snap as the Irish operate out
of the shotgun.

"I didn't have time to be nervous. If we didn't do it, I
wasn't going to worry. It's the second game of the season,"
said Kiel later. The previous game Kiel had played in was the
Indiana All-State Game where he had been named the most
valuable player.

The first play isolates Hunter on defensive back Body. The
ball looks like a rainbow as it arches across the field. Hunter is
in front of the Michigan bench as he stretches his 6'5"
frame up for the ball. For a moment, Body comes in contact
with Hunter, immediately a flag is hurled to the ground, and
pass interference is whistled. Schembechler is livid, stomping
the ground as he berates the official. When later asked about
the call, Schembechler remarked, "No comment."

It's first down for the Irish at the Wolverine 48. The pass
play took ten seconds. Kiel goes for Holohan on first down,
but the attempt is broken up. Masztak drops the second-down
pass, but Kiel is successful to Carter, out of the backfield, and
nine yards are picked up. The tailback, who has gained 103
yards on the day, nearly wastes too much time as he tries to
stop the clock. On fourth down Kiel finds Hunter on the

west sideline. Hunter is confused after making the catch and turns the wrong way, back toward the field, but his foot touches the chalk of the sideline, and he is out of bounds with four seconds left in the game. The stage is set for one of the most dramatic plays in Irish football history.

A constant wind has been blowing over the south end of the stadium. It has made the game one of big plays and position football. The first two Irish scores were with the wind as was the go-ahead Michigan score. The wind is now not as steady as it had been in the third quarter and comes in quiet gusts, picking at the flags that hang on top of the stadium.

The Irish must go for the field goal of fifty-one yards. Cichy would be the most likely candidate, but an injured neck has kept him out of the game. Johnston has better range than Oliver but the ball is marked on the right hash. As the left-footed, soccer-style kicker would hit the ball, his natural motion would swing the ball from left to right. The natural hook would make it easier for Oliver to connect and pull the ball back through the uprights. Another point in Oliver's favor is the low trajectory that a soccer-style booter has. With the wind playing tricks, the ball has a better chance of cutting into the breeze, but there is also a better chance of a block.

Oliver is the choice of the coaching staff. He has been consistent, save the missed extra point. The holder is Tim Koegel. Both players attended Cincinnati's Moeller High School. Bill Siewe would make the crucial snap.

During the Michigan touchdown drive, Oliver had prepared himself for what would come. "I was just trying to keep my leg loose. I was also praying on the sideline. I was asking, 'Mary, may the best thing happen.' "

It could not happen better. The snap from Siewe is perfect, as is Koegel's hold. Oliver swings his leg, and the ball is airborne. It appears to pause, then turn over and gain speed. The descent is agonizingly slow, then another jolt of speed propels the ball earthward. Fans at the base of the southern goalpost peer upward as the ball falls through the uprights for the biggest field goal in Notre Dame history.

The kick is headed for the south end of Notre Dame stadium as Harry Oliver follows through with the winner against the Wolverines. Tim Koegel's finger is still in the holding position. Notice Oliver's head, still down, concentrating on the kick.

Pandemonium. Ecstasy. Dejection. Anger. Sorrow. Elation. The gamut of emotion is seen on the field. Teammates rush to mob their hero. Oliver can't believe that he has kicked the longest field goal of his life. Michigan has seen victory flee on the instep of Harry Oliver.

"I didn't even see it," said Oliver after receiving the game ball. "But Tim jumped on me and was telling me, 'It's good! It's good.'

"This is by far the greatest moment of my life. Getting a scholarship to Notre Dame was a close second." Oliver would not have gone over well in the 1960s. He is about as ordinary as one can be. But he is also honest. When he speaks of his devotion to his faith and to the Blessed Virgin, he is totally sincere.

"I have to thank God; God had to be with me. My teammates are the greatest; they supported me and I love every one of them."

Dan Devine had again captured a win when all appeared

The celebration is on! Oliver cannot believe that he has beaten Michigan with a 51-yard field goal as time expires. Tim Koegel (14) and Pete Buchanan (35) rush to embrace Oliver.

lost. Fighting to overcome tears in a tearful locker room, Devine recalled the kick.

"I knew right away that it was true and that he kicked it good. . . . I've never seen Oliver kick one that far, but it went through today, and that's all I care about."

Schembechler was terse as he talked about the game. He was asked about his change of quarterbacks after the Krimm touchdown.

Oliver is ushered off the field by All-America defensive end Scott Zettek and defensive tackle Pat Kramer.

"The decision was mine. . . . Our quarterback situation is fluid–it could be anybody." Schembechler was then asked about Oliver's kick. "He hit it good," muttered Bo.

Nearly lost in the shuffle was Blair Kiel. He had marched the Irish into position for the winning score and had not really grasped the magnitude of the situation. "I didn't know if he [Devine] was going to bring me in or not. At the very last minute when they were getting ready to score, that is when they told me I was going in."

Kiel was also gracious about Mike Courey. "He's the one that led them all the way in the first place. He was encouraging me. When you've got the whole team backing you, you just can't go wrong."

Both coaches were proud of their teams' efforts. Schembechler told his team that it was a great Michigan effort. "When two great schools like this get together, you expect this kind of game. Notre Dame is a great team, and we like to play against them," said Bo.

Devine's remarks were similar: "We beat a good football team and had to come from behind to do it. That's gotta do something for our boys. Michigan is an excellent football team; I have to give them a lot of credit."

The greatness continued for both squads in 1980. Notre Dame was ranked no. 1 midway through the season and received a bid to the Sugar Bowl, losing to National Champion Georgia. Michigan finally beat the bowl-game jinx. After losing the week after the Irish game, the Wolverines reeled off nine straight wins, capped off by a resounding defeat of Washington in the Rose Bowl.

Michigan and Notre Dame in 1980 was a dream game. Just as Rod Bone had dreamed of Krimm's interception return for a score, Harry Oliver made it a dream come true for Irish fans. The mystique that surrounds the school received a boost and credibility once again. Perhaps defensive tackle Pat Kramer said it best: "This could only happen here."

REFERENCES

Reference material for this book came from a variety of sources. The Notre Dame Sports Information office provided official game notes, including the play-by-play of each game. Quotes from many of the principals in each game are contained within the official game notes. When possible individual interviews were conducted. The following is a list of print and electronic source material.

Books

Gildea, William, and Jennison, Christopher. *The Fighting Irish*. Englewood Cliffs, NJ: Prentice-Hall, 1976.
Izenberg, Jerry. *The Rivals*. New York: Holt, Rinehart and Winston, 1968.
Layden, Elmer with Ed Snyder. *It Was a Different Game*. Englewood Cliffs, NJ: Prentice-Hall, 1969.
Pagna, Tom, and Best, Bob. *Era of Ara*. Huntsville, AL: Strode, 1967.
Twombley, Wells. *Shake Down the Thunder*. Radnor, PA: Chilton Books, 1976.

Newspapers and Periodicals

Associated Press, Nov. 3, 1935. "Notre Dame-Ohio State." Alan Gould.

Chicago Sun-Times, Nov. 22, 1953; Jan. 1, 1974; Sept. 21, 1980.

Chicago Tribune, Nov. 22, 1953; Nov. 20, 1966; Jan. 2, 1979.

NRTA Journal, Nov.-Dec. 1978. "Football's Greatest Game." Tim Cohane.

New York Sun, Nov. 3, 1913.

New York Times, Nov. 3, 1913.

Notre Dame Observer, Dec. 1, 1970.

Notre Dame Scholastic, Nov. 1, 1935.

Notre Dame Scholastic Football Review, 1966, 1970, 1974, 1979.

South Bend News-Times, Nov. 3, 1913.

South Bend Tribune, Nov. 22, 1953; Nov. 20, 1966; Jan. 1, 1974; Oct. 14, 1975; Jan. 2, 1979; Oct. 28, 1979; Sept. 21, 1980.

Ohio State Lantern, Oct. 31, 1935.

United Press, Nov. 3, 1935. "Notre Dame-Ohio State." Tommy Devine.

United Press, Nov. 3, 1935. "Notre Dame-Ohio State." H. McLemore.

Washington Star, Nov. 3, 1935.

Television

The Comeback Kid. Tom F. Dennin, Exec. Producer. WNDU-TV, South Bend, IN, 1979.

The Devine Years. Tom F. Dennin, Exec. Producer. WNDU-TV, South Bend, IN, 1981.

INDEX